Rosalie Mackinnon.

NEEDLEWORK

This book was selected for inclusion in the
British Book Production Exhibition of books
published in 1959, with the description: 'An
example of the care and imagination which
Methuen and some other publishers are spend-
ing on schoolbooks. An attractive binding, and
a system of headings which combines style
with clarity.'

ROSALIE P. GILES

holds City and Guilds 1st Class
Teacher's Certificates in Dress-
making, Needlework and Cookery.
She is a teacher in the Catering and
Domestic Science Department of
the Norwich City College and Art
School

ROSALIE P. GILES

NEEDLE-
WORK

LONDON
METHUEN & CO LTD
36 ESSEX STREET WC2

FIRST PUBLISHED 3rd DECEMBER, 1959
REPRINTED TWICE 1960
REPRINTED 1961 AND 1963
1.5
© 1959 ROSALIE P. GILES
PRINTED IN GREAT BRITAIN BY
COX & WYMAN LTD
FAKENHAM
CAT. NO. 2/8174/6 (SCHOOL EDITION)
2/6135/5 (BEST EDITION)

Contents

CONTENTS

Foreword

In this book I have tried to meet the requirements of the G.C.E. Ordinary Level and the Royal Society of Arts School Certificate syllabuses for Needlework. It should be suitable for use in Secondary Modern Schools, Grammar Schools, evening classes and for students working for the City and Guilds examinations in Needlework.

I should like to take this opportunity to express my gratitude to Mrs. K. Thaxton for permission to use her method of inserting the gusset in a magyar sleeve, and to Miss L. Papworth for introducing me to the publishers.

My thanks are due to Dr H. W. Howes, C.M.G., O.B.E., M.A., M.Sc., formerly Director of Education in Ceylon and Gibraltar and at present Director of Education for British Honduras. As a former student of his when Dr Howes was Principal of Norwich City College and Art School before he went abroad, I am indebted to him, but more particularly for the encouragement and advice he gave me when this book was being prepared.

R. P. G.

The following abbreviations
are used throughout this book

C.B. centre back
C.F. centre front
R.S. right side
W.S. wrong side

1: Needlework Equipment and its care and use

Needlework is a fascinating and satisfying craft while being, at the same time, a most useful and essential one. In this machine age there is still great scope for skill in handwork as well as in the use of the many machines now on the market. Great pleasure can be derived from making clothes, and much expense saved, while the modern machine speeds up and takes the drudgery out of repair work, making both clothes and household articles last longer. This is a craft every girl should learn and she will never regret the time spent in acquiring the knowledge of it.

Before attempting any craft one must have the right tools, and needlework is no exception. Buy the best that can be afforded and look after it well and it will last a long time. The essential equipment needed will be as follows:

Scissors

A pair of good cutting-out scissors about 8″ long. A smaller pair for cutting cotton and buttonholes. A small pair with both ends pointed for embroidery. Never use scissors for any purpose other than that for which they are intended and keep them sharpened always.

Needles

Have a good assorted supply. Needles are numbered for size, high numbers for fine ones and low numbers for the coarser types.

For ordinary sewing use 'sharps' size 8.

For fine sewing use 'betweens' size 8. 'Betweens' are shorter than 'sharps' but are the same thickness round.

Darning. Use a darning needle. These are long and have large eyes. The size will depend on the thickness of the thread being used. These needles are useful for tailor tacking as fresh lengths of cotton are frequently needed and the large eye makes constant threading easy.

For embroidery use crewel needles which are short and have large eyes for easy threading.

Pins

Use dressmakers' *steel* pins. These are bluish in colour and have sharp points which do not damage or mark the material. The very small lill pins are useful, sometimes, for fine work. Do not keep pins in a tin, for the action of the metal on the pins makes them dirty. A pincushion is the most satisfactory way of keeping them clean and free from rust.

Bodkin

This is like a large needle with a blunt end and is used for threading elastic and for turning out rouleau.

Thimble

White metal thimbles give the longest wear, silver ones are too soft and too easily pierced. A thimble should fit comfortably.

Tape Measure

This should be of good quality, otherwise it will stretch. If no hem-marker is available, a yardstick is useful for levelling hems.

Pressing Equipment

Irons should be comfortable to handle and should weigh about seven pounds. One which can be regulated may be left with no fear of scorching. Steam irons are light in weight but are useful for pressing velvet, woollens, nylon and embroidery and for the final pressing of garments, as they create steam overcoming the need for a damping cloth. However, when pressing seams in heavy materials, the damping cloth is still needed to obtain a really flat finish. For the pressing cloth use about one yard of sheeting or tailor's canvas from which all the dressing has been washed out.

The ironing board should be a comfortable height; some can be adjusted. It should be padded with felt and covered with a loose cover made of white drill.

Thread

Choose a thread suitable for the work in hand as follows:

For tacking use size 60 tacking cotton and for tailor tacking size 40. This cotton is a cheaper, inferior type which is slightly fluffy and enables tailor tacks to stay in the material.

For sewing cotton material use cotton size 40 for ordinary work and size 80 for fine work. If the colour cannot be matched in cotton, use sylko.

For rayon material use sylko size 40. This is a cotton thread which has been treated to give it a sheen.

For linen use pure sewing silk.

For silk and woollen materials use pure sewing silk as it is slightly elastic and 'gives' with the stretch in the material and so is not likely to break in wear.

Nylon and terylene. Very fine but strong nylon and terylene threads are made for use with these materials.

Machine darning. Use the very fine darning cotton made especially for the purpose.

The Sewing Machine

This is the most expensive piece of equipment but a sound investment, as it more than pays for itself in a short time. Whether it is the more humble kind with a long shuttle or the exciting supermatic type, a sewing machine is a joy to use and, if much sewing is done, an electric one saves the most time and leaves both hands free to manipulate the work. One's sewing machine becomes an old friend and should be treated as such. Given proper care and usage it should last a lifetime.

TO CLEAN AND OIL THE MACHINE

If the machine is used daily, oil it after every ten hours use but if used less frequently, about once a month.

1) Unscrew the throat plate underneath the needle and remove it.

2) Using a small brush with stiff bristles, brush out all accumulated fluff and dust from the bobbin case and round the feed dog. Replace the plate and screw it down again.

3) Oil all moving parts and never let the oil dry on them. The positions of the oiling points will be shown in the instruction booklet supplied with the machine. Turn the machine back on its hinges and oil the points underneath; also clean out any fluff and pins which may be there.

4) Run the machine rapidly for a short while with no cotton threaded in it. This helps the oil to soak in.

5) Wipe off any surplus oil and dust the machine with a non-fluffy cloth. When not in use leave a piece of material under the needle to soak up any oil which may run down it. Keep the lid on the machine.

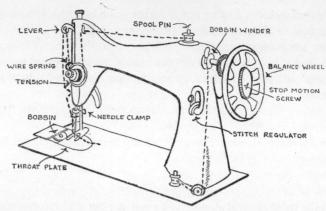

The diagram above shows the main parts of a sewing machine.

The stop motion screw puts the needle out of action when it is turned towards the worker and this is usually done when filling the bobbin.

The stitch regulator adjusts the length of the stitch. For ordinary work set it at 12 stitches to the inch and at 16 for fine work.

The tension and wire spring control the tightness of the stitch, which should look exactly the same on the top side as on the underside. The top and bottom threads must be of the same thickness and should link together in the centre of the work, see diagram. If the stitches on the underside are looped, check the top threading and, if there is no fault here, turn the tension wheel to the right to

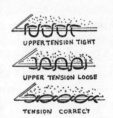

tighten the stitch. Should the stitches on the top side loop, check the threading of the bobbin case.

The needle may have one side of the shank flat and the other rounded or it may be completely rounded, according to the model. One side of the needle has a long groove running down to the eye and the other side a short one. The cotton is always threaded through from the side with the long groove and this is opposite the flat side of the shank. When it is necessary to change the needle, turn it to its highest point and unscrew the clamp. Remove the needle and insert the new one as far up as it will go, then re-tighten the screw. As in some machines the needle is threaded from the right to the left and in others the reverse way, make sure that it is put in with the long groove to the side from which it is threaded. For general work use a

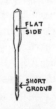

size 14 needle and a size 11 for fine work. The instruction booklet will give directions for threading the particular type of machine.

Most machines are driven by a belt which must be correctly adjusted, for if it is too tight the machine is hard to work and if too loose, the belt slips. Should it stretch in wear it can be unhooked and shortened.

REASONS FOR FAULTS IN MACHINING

Cotton breaking

1) The tension may be too tight.
2) The needle may be in the wrong way round.
3) The cotton may become wound round the spool pin under the reel or, it may have become caught in the slit in the reel.
4) The needle may be too fine or too coarse for the thread.

Skipped stitches

1) The needle may be too small for the thread.
2) The needle may not be correctly inserted.

Puckered material

1) The needle may be too large for fine material.
2) The needle may be blunt.
3) The tension may be too tight.

Looped stitches

1) The tension may need adjusting.
2) The bobbin case may not be threaded correctly.

RULES FOR USING THE SEWING MACHINE

1) As far as possible, keep the bulk of the work to the left of the machine, as it is more easily handled this way.
2) There must be ample table space to the left for the work to rest on comfortably.
3) Before inserting material into the machine make sure the needle and bobbin threads are pulled under the presser foot towards the back. This prevents them from becoming tangled when stitching begins.
4) To begin stitching, place the work in position and lower the needle into it, then lower the presser foot.
5) To withdraw the work raise the needle to its highest point, raise the presser foot and pull the material towards the back of the machine.

Cut the threads, leaving ends at least 3″ long in the machine to prevent the needle from becoming unthreaded when stitching is resumed.

6) The presser foot may be used as a guide for keeping machining straight, as, for instance, when stitching overlaid seams by keeping the edge of the seam level with the inside of the right hand part of the foot. For parallel rows of decorative stitching, use the foot as a guide for keeping the width between the rows accurate.

The foot is useful also as a guide for the width and spacing of small tucks. See diagrams.

EDGE STITCHING

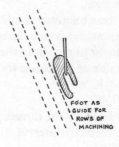

FOOT AS
GUIDE FOR
ROWS OF
MACHINING

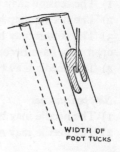

WIDTH OF
FOOT TUCKS

7) Before turning a corner, put the needle well down into the material to keep it in position while turning.

8) After removing work from the machine, fasten off the ends securely. Draw both threads through to the wrong side of the work, thread them into a needle, and run back for a short distance into

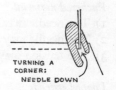

TURNING A
CORNER:
NEEDLE DOWN

the stitching. Some machines have a reverse which enables the needle to run backwards over the stitches already formed, thus saving time.

The more recently introduced swing needle machines open up a wide field for machining, as they are able to stitch automatically many embroidery stitches which give plenty of scope for individual designing. They save much time by automatically oversewing seams and are ideal for stitching very fine seams in nylon fabrics.

II: Choosing Materials and Styles

Apart from being so useful, needlework can be so exciting. It is very interesting to make clothes for oneself and for others, for each garment is an adventure which has to suit an individual's personality, colouring and build, as well as being suitable for the purpose for which it is intended. This is what is meant by being well dressed—being suitable in all respects. Study the individual carefully—is she tall or short, dark or fair, gay and light-hearted or of a more serious nature? It is just as much in bad taste to make a frilly, fluffy style for a severe personality as it is to choose an elaborate and 'dressy' garment to wear for every day work. Look for people's good points and draw attention to them—look for their bad points and try to disguise them and lead the eye away from them.

Colours

Choose a colour carefully—not just because it is attractive or the fashion for the moment, for it may not suit the person who is to wear it or it may not 'go' with her existing clothes and accessories.

Fair people with fair skins can wear any colour successfully. If the eyes are a good feature select a colour which will accentuate them. People with sallow skins look best, as a rule, in pure bright colours which act as a contrast. High coloured complexions can be toned down by the reflected light from cool colours such as greens and ice blues. These colours also act as a good contrast to auburn hair. Elderly people look dignified and graceful in pastel shades, but remember that light colours tend to enlarge, while dark colours are slimming and help to flatter the outsize figure.

The choice of accessories is as important as the choice of the garment, and they may tone with it or be in contrast to it. Hats, gloves, scarves and shoes look smart when they all match but are a muddle if they are of different colours, or of different tones of the same colour.

B

Texture

Materials may be smooth, rough or fluffy, dull or shiny, and this texture is important. Outsize people should avoid the use of shiny materials such as satin and some velvets which catch the light on curves and give the appearance of increased size. Thin people look well in rough, knobbly or fluffy textures which give them bulk.

Get into the habit of judging materials by the feel and weight of them. Loosely woven materials may stretch and 'seat' in wear and then shrink when cleaned. Very wiry materials and some very light ones which have no substance may not drape well. The texture must be considered in relation to the style chosen, for bulky material is not suitable for gathering and some crease resisting materials do not always pleat satisfactorily.

Patterned Material

Patterns on materials also play their part. Anyone can wear stripes provided they run in the right direction. Vertical stripes are slimming and give height, therefore they are suitable for short and outsize figures. Horizontal stripes give an appearance of width and reduce the height and so are best worn by the thin and the tall. Small patterns suit the petite figure and large patterns help to reduce height. On the whole, patterned materials are more slimming than light plain ones as the eye is attracted to the pattern rather than to the figure. Large check and plaid patterns are only becoming to the average and slim figure and they are not suitable for dresses which are cut into many panels owing to the impossibility of matching the pattern everywhere.

The cut and style of a dress can do much to disguise bad points. For example, very round faces appear longer if V and low neck lines are chosen, and people with long faces should wear high necks and collars. For the top-heavy figure with a large bust, keep the bodice plain and concentrate the interest in the skirt, as this draws the eye downwards away from the bust. Large hips are less noticeable if the bodice fits loosely and the interest is across the shoulders drawing the eye upwards. Plan gathering over a flat bust.

Vertical lines, as in the princess type and button through dresses, are slimming and should be chosen for the larger figure. This type of figure should never be overfitted.

Gathered and very flared skirts suit the average, slim and petite figures—the latter can also wear frills and flounces successfully. Larger figures look better in straight or draped skirts.

Planning Wardrobes

Always buy the expensive items, such as top coats and suits, first and then plan the less expensive items to wear with them. A loose coat is useful for most occasions and if it matches the suit, the two can be worn together for warmth when needed. If a fairly neutral colour is chosen, variety can be introduced by different coloured sets of blouses, scarves, hats, gloves and handbags, as and when they can be afforded. In this way the larger items last longer without one tiring of them. A plain suit is of more use as plain, patterned and frilly blouses can be worn with it, whereas a patterned suit ties one down to plain blouses only.

By all means be in fashion but avoid extremes which 'date' a garment so that its life is short although it may not be worn out.

Use jewellery very carefully, especially during the daytime, as it can be so easily overdone and look out of place.

Children's clothes should be:

1) Attractive in colour and pattern to the child as well as to the parent.
2) Non-inflammable, hardwearing and able to withstand frequent washing.
3) Warm and light in weight as heavy clothes are tiring.
4) Comfortable with plenty of room for movement.

CLASSIFICATION OF MATERIALS AND THEIR SUITABILITY FOR DIFFERENT PURPOSES

Materials may be divided into three groups, animal, vegetable and man-made.

1. Animal Fibres

WOOL

This is obtained from sheep, goats, camels and rabbits.

Under a microscope a woollen fibre appears to have tiny overlapping scales or projections and, when woven or knitted these projections entangle air between them. This air acts as an insulator and helps to keep warmth in the body. Loosely woven or knitted materials give greater warmth than close heavy ones as they have larger spaces to entrap air. For this reason wool is a bad conductor of heat as it keeps warmth in the body instead of conducting it away, and is, therefore, suitable for wearing in cold weather.

WOOL FIBRE

Because wool is able to absorb considerable amounts of moisture it is often used for garments worn after playing strenuous games to absorb perspiration and so lessen the danger of getting chills. Wool is light in weight and soft to wear and it is non-inflammable for it does not catch alight but only chars slowly, making it safe for children's wear. It is made in many weights suitable for most types of garment, from underwear to heavy outer coats. Often it is mixed with other fibres, such as Terylene, to make it crease resistant, or with cotton to make it stronger and cheaper. The only disadvantages are that it is expensive, liable to be attacked by moth grubs and is inclined to shrink and felt up if carelessly laundered. When this happens the projecting scales become interlocked and no longer entrap air, making the material thick and less warm.

Most woollen materials such as gabardine, alpaca, wool jersey, barathea, tweeds, velour cloth and light-weight dress materials are 54″ wide but flannel and Harris tweed are 27″ wide.

Test for wool. To make sure a material is pure wool, burn a small piece and it should smoulder, form a black bead and smell like burnt hair.

SILK

The silkworm exudes a sticky liquid which solidifies into silken threads. The thread may be up to 4,000 yards long and the insect winds it round itself to form a cocoon. When the moth is ready to emerge it softens one end of the cocoon with liquid and bores its way out. This, of course, spoils the silk, so the cocoon is subjected to steam to kill the insect before it can do this. About a quarter of the silk can be wound off in a continuous thread. The rest breaks and is spun into thread for making spun silk which is much cheaper than the best silks.

Next to nylon, silk is the strongest thread and it may be woven or knitted. Materials made from it are absorbent and warm, have a lovely lustre and are very pleasant to handle. They drape beautifully and have a certain amount of elasticity which makes them very suitable for lingerie, blouses and dresses.

Sometimes silken materials are weighted—that is, treated with a chemical dressing to give them substance. If there is a lot of this weighting the material may rot quickly.

To test if a material is pure silk, burn a scrap and it should melt slowly into a black bead and smell like burnt feathers. If the material is weighted it glows, does not form the bead and does not smell.

Silk materials are usually 36″ wide and are expensive.

2. Vegetable Fibres

COTTON

Cotton fibres come from the hairy seeds of cotton plants and seen under a microscope they are flat and twisted. The twist makes them strong and elastic.

Cotton is cool to wear and takes up moisture easily but does not hold it as wool does, so that when perspiration evaporates in the course of drying, heat is withdrawn from the body; therefore, cotton is a good conductor of heat and is suitable for summer wear. It is light in weight, strong, comparatively cheap and stands up to a lot of wear and laundering. It is very suitable for overalls, shirts, dresses, sports' wear, children's clothes and household articles.

COTTON FIBRE

Cotton materials are lawn, calico, drill, cambric, gingham, piqué, seersucker, poplin, Tobralco, organdie, muslin, lace, corduroy, velveteen and winceyette. The last named has a fluffed up surface which entraps air and makes it warmer. Its use for children's nightwear is not recommended as it is highly inflammable. Mercerised cotton, such as poplin and sylko sewing thread, is treated with caustic soda to give it a sheen. Most cotton materials are 36″ wide except velveteen and corduroy which may be only 27″ wide.

To test for cotton, burn it and it should flare up quickly and leave little ash.

LINEN

Linen comes from the stems of the flax plant and is stronger and heavier than cotton. It is a smooth, round and lustrous fibre, notched at intervals. Linen materials are good conductors of heat and are cool to wear. They are strong and wear well and are made in various weights from fine cambric used for blouses, to fine smooth linens used for church and household linen, to the heavier types which are suitable for dresses and summer suits. Linen is rather expensive and the width varies from 36″ to 48″ or 54″. The burning test is the same as for cotton.

LINEN FIBRE

3. Man-made Fibres

RAYON

This material is made from cellulose which is the fleshy parts of plants. It is not produced naturally as are wool and silk, but is treated and manufactured by man. There are three main types of rayon thread; viscose, acetate and cuprammonium.

1) *Viscose rayon* is made from wood pulp chemically treated with caustic soda and carbon disulphide to reduce it to a thick, sticky, orange coloured liquid which is forced through tiny holes in a spinning jet into fine continuous threads, or filaments, which harden on exposure to air and are then further hardened with sulphuric acid. The thickness of the threads depends on the size of the holes on the spinneret. As the threads harden they are twisted together to form the yarn. Viscose rayons are absorbent and good conductors of heat. They drape well and are moth proof.

2) *Acetate rayon* is made from cotton linters which are treated with acetic acid and acetic anhydride and dried into flakes which are then dissolved in acetone into a sticky white liquid. This is forced through the spinning jet and solidified in a current of warm air. The threads are twisted together to form the yarn which is made into attractive materials with good draping qualities, giving long wear. They are absorbent, crease resisting and moth proof. They should be washed carefully in warm water and ironed with a cool iron. Heat and chemicals damage them. Celanese is made from this yarn. Tricel is a development of acetate rayon which is very strong and crease resistant and can be durably pleated. It dries quickly and needs little ironing.

3) *Cuprammonium* is also made from cotton linters which are dissolved in copper sulphate, ammonia and soda. The filaments are hardened in a chemical bath and become elastic. They are then drawn out to the required degree of fineness.

FILAMENT AND STAPLE YARNS

Rayon yarn may be an unending continuous filament which is woven into smooth, lustrous fabrics such as taffetas, poults and satins. Materials are also made from rayon staple which consists of filament yarn cut into short lengths and spun together into a yarn which produces heavier, warmer materials. According to the way in which it is spun, many different fabrics can be made from this yarn, examples being, suitings, velvets, dress and furnishing brocades. Rayon yarn is naturally lustrous but can be treated to give a dull surface.

Rayons are usually 36″ wide but furnishing fabrics may be 54″ wide. They often resemble silk but are much less expensive and are well within the reach of most people.

When the burning test is applied, acetate rayon melts into a black bead and other rayons flare up like cotton leaving no ash.

PROTEIN FIBRES

Aralac and Fibrolane are made from the protein of milk. They are soft, warm and absorbent and for this reason are often mixed with nylon and cotton to give these materials the qualities they lack. They do not irritate the skin and are useful for underwear and nightwear.

NYLON

This is a completely synthetic fibre manufactured from coal, water and air (oxygen and nitrogen) from which small polymer chips are obtained. These are melted into a sticky liquid, forced through fine jets and solidified by air. The fibre is very elastic and is drawn out to the required degree of fineness. It may be used as continuous filament or as staple yarn to make a great many types of fabric from fine chiffon and Tricot to knitting yarn and fur fabric. Its elasticity makes it suitable for stockings.

The qualities of nylon :
1) It is extremely strong although it is light in weight and sometimes looks delicate.
2) As a rule it is non-inflammable. When it is burnt it melts away from the flame into a black sticky substance which hardens when it is cooled.
3) It is moth proof, rot proof and crease resistant.
4) It washes easily, dries quickly and needs little or no ironing. For these reasons nylon garments are ideal for packing and travelling as they always look crisp and fresh.
5) It may be mixed with other fibres to give them strength and crease resistance and to enable them to be durably pleated.

The disadvantages are :
1) Nylon is not absorbent and the fineness of the thread in some materials makes the weave so close that perspiration can be neither soaked up nor evaporated which may be uncomfortable. This difficulty may be overcome by making these garments from nylon Tricot or open mesh nylon which have air spaces giving an outlet.
2) Nylon becomes charged with static electricity which causes it to pick up and hold dirt. The hems of petticoats are particularly affected by this and frequent laundering is essential to prevent permanent discolouration.
3) It is damaged by some acids and bleaches and by strong sunlight which makes it unsuitable for curtains.

TERYLENE

A synthetic fibre discovered in 1941, Terylene polymer chips are made
from substances which are obtained from petroleum. They are melted
and made into threads in the same way as nylon. In England it is
manufactured by Imperial Chemical Industries Ltd and in America
it is made under the name of Dacron.

Terylene has much the same properties as nylon but is not so elastic
and on account of this, was for a time, unsuitable for making stockings
but the difficulty has been overcome. It is softer and drapes more
satisfactorily than nylon and is resistant to sunlight and therefore
suitable for curtains. It does not shrink and can be durably pleated.

The disadvantages are that it is expensive and it is liable to slippage,
the threads slipping on top of each other and looking as if they have
pulled away at the seams.

ORLON

Another synthetic fabric with bulking power, as it can be fluffed up to
entrap air and resembles wool but is not so absorbent. It is not so
strong as Terylene but is soft, fleecy and warm and drapes well.

NYLON AND TERYLENE IN NEEDLEWORK

1) Both fray badly and turnings $\frac{3}{4}''$ wide must be allowed. It is helpful
to use pinking shears for cutting out, allowing still wider turnings as
the pinking will have to be trimmed off when the seams are neatened.
Always use sharp scissors and never tear these materials.
2) Use Terylene thread for stitching as the fibres are so strong they
can cut through cotton.
3) Use size 10 sewing needles and size 9 for machine needles, as the
threads are so fine that thicker needles cannot penetrate between them
and may cause puckering. Machine stitches must be small, 20–30 to
the inch. Loosen the tension and feed the work gently through without
forcing it, otherwise it will pucker.
4) Use French seams when possible not less than $\frac{1}{4}''$ wide. Plain seams
must be neatened with edge stitching, close oversewing or better still
with machine oversewing.

PLASTIC MATERIALS

These are used for aprons, toilet bags and curtains. As curtains they
are not very hygienic as no air can pass through. They can be neither
pinned nor tacked but seams may be held together for stitching with

paper clips of the sliding variety. Place tissue paper under the plastic when machining to prevent the feed of the machine marking it on the underside. After stitching tear the paper away. As stitching perforates, and so weakens, the plastic use a long machine stitch, about 8 to the inch. Wherever possible strengthen all edges with crossway binding.

The Structure of Fabrics

There are three main ways in which materials are made, namely by felting, knitting and weaving.

Felting. This method, in which fibres are matted together, is used for making felt and Vilene, an interlining material used for stiffening revers, collars, belts, etc.

Knitting. All fibres except linen are suitable for knitting and many fabrics are made in this way, examples being jersey cloth, rayon locknit and nylon tricot. Sometimes these materials are tubular, making cutting out more economical.

Woven fabrics. In this method, parallel threads, called warp threads, arc arranged on a loom and, by means of a shuttle, other threads, called weft threads, are interlaced backwards and forwards across them. At either side the weft threads form a finished edge which is called the selvedge edge. In needlework this edge is usually cut off as it is woven more tightly than the rest of the material and is inclined to shrink more. If it has to be used, it should be clipped across at intervals. When the selvedge edge has been cut off, the warp may be distinguished from the weft in the following ways:

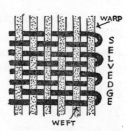

1) If the material is torn across both ways it should be harder to tear across the selvedge than with it.

2) The torn ends of the weft threads are short and close together; those of the warp are longer and more widely and evenly spaced.

3) The warp threads are usually thicker and stronger than the weft.

The Grain of the Material

The warp and weft threads are called the 'straight grain' of the material. It is usual to cut patterns out so that the warp runs down a garment as the material wears better this way.

When the material is cut diagonally across the warp and weft threads at an angle of 45° it is said to be on 'the cross'. Cut this way, material is very elastic.

The Nap of the Material

Some materials, such as velveteens and velvets, have a raised surface or pile. This feels rough one way and smooth the other when stroked, and it looks darker one way than the other. The darker way is the correct way up and silk velvets usually smooth upwards on a garment and velveteens and corduroys downwards. When cutting out, all pattern pieces must be placed on the material with the pile or nap running in the right direction and this is often wasteful.

Materials which have a pattern running in one direction only are said to have nap. When the material is plain or has a pattern running in all directions so that it does not matter if parts of the pattern are turned upside down for economical cutting, it is said to have no nap.

In the long run it pays to buy the best quality material that can be afforded. Choose it carefully, bearing in mind all the time, the style of the pattern, the purpose for which it is intended and the amount of wear and tear it will have to withstand.

The Quantity of Material Needed for Garments

BLOUSES

Allow twice the length from the nape to the waist + 14" for the tuck in and hem + ¾ yd. for long and ½ yd. for short sleeves.

SKIRTS

Twice the length + 5" for hems and turnings. Very full or elaborate skirts require more material and it must be calculated from the pattern.

DRESSES

Twice the length from nape to hem + 5" for hems and turnings + ¾ yd. for long or ½ yd. for short sleeves. If the hips are large or the skirt full allow an extra skirt length.

OVERALLS

Twice the length + 5" for hems and turnings + ¾ yd. for long or ½ yd. for short sleeves + ¼ yd. for the collar and belt.

HOUSECOATS AND DRESSING GOWNS

Three times the total length + 5" for hems and turnings + ¾ yd. for long or ½ yd. for short sleeves.

NIGHTDRESSES

Twice the length + 5" for hems and turnings + ¾ yd. for long and ½ yd for short sleeves.

PYJAMAS

Twice the length of the jacket + 5" and twice the length of the trousers + 5" + ¾ yd. for long or ½ yd. for short sleeves.

PETTICOATS

Twice the length + 5" for hems.

KNICKERS

Twice the length + 5" for hems.

BRASSIERES

Three-eighths of a yard if of single material and ¾ yd. if double.

The above calculations are based on material 36" wide. The amount needed if the material is 54" wide is estimated as follows:
If 3 yds. of 36" material is needed divide 36 by 54 and multiply by 3.

$$\frac{36 \times 3}{54} = 2 \text{ yds.}$$

If a material has a large check or plaid pattern, or stripes which must be matched allow ¾ yd. more. More material may be required if it has a nap running in one direction only and the actual amount is best calculated by laying the pattern pieces out and measuring them.

III: The Pattern

There are three ways of obtaining a pattern.

1) By making a block pattern to an individual's measurements. This is drafted to certain measurements taken from the body and should be a perfect fit. It is used as a basis for making patterns for any style required.

2) By modelling. The material is actually draped on the figure in the style required and then cut out.

3) By buying a trade pattern. It is *NO* economy to try to save money on this pattern. Buy the very best you can afford. The money is well spent, for a good pattern goes together accurately, gives little trouble in fitting and the style is usually in good taste.

Trade patterns are cut to average standard measurements which have been worked out from the individual measurements of many people. The measurements of the person for whom a garment is being made, must be compared with those of the pattern, for they may not *ALL* be the same, and, in this event the pattern will have to be adjusted.

Measurements are taken in the following way:

The Bodice

1) BUST Take this measurement round the fullest part of the bust with two fingers inside the tape measure. Keep the tape high up under the arms at the back.

2) FRONT WIDTH Taken across the front from where the sleeves are set in and at a level of 4″ below the nape of the neck.

3) FRONT LENGTH Take this from the neck end of the shoulder to the centre front of a tape tied round the waist.

4) WAIST Taken round the natural waist. Push the tape measure well down.

5) ACROSS BACK WIDTH Taken across the back from where the

sleeves are set in at a level of 4″ below the nape bone.

6) BACK LENGTH Taken from the nape bone to the centre back of a tape tied round the waist.

The Sleeve

7) SLEEVE LENGTH Take this from the top of the shoulder, over the bent elbow and up to the wrist.
8) SLEEVE WIDTH Take this round the developed biceps muscle and add 2″ for ease.
9) WRIST Taken round the wrist for a sleeve with an opening. For a sleeve without an opening take this measurement round the clenched fist.

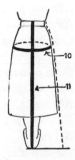

The Skirt

10) HIP MEASUREMENT Taken round the hips 7″ below the waist.

11) SKIRT LENGTH Take this at the centre back and front and also at the sides from the waist down to the ground. Deduct the fashionable length from the ground from the resulting measurements, which may not be all the same depending on the individual figure.

12) KNICKER LENGTH This is taken in a sitting position from the waist to the required leg length.

Bodice Block Pattern

The measurements needed for the bodice are:
1) Back length from the nape to the waist.
2) Across back width.
3) Across front width.
4) The bust.
5) The waist.

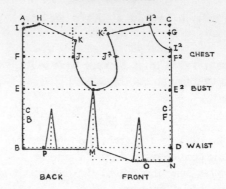

Construction lines (marked with dots) Only half the pattern is drafted.

AB = the back length plus $\frac{1}{2}''$.

AC = half the bust plus $1''$ for ease.

CD = AB and BD = AC. Draw a rectangle.

AE = $8\frac{1}{2}''$ always. Square a line across from E to E^2.

AF = half AE. Square across from F to F^2.

CG = a quarter of AF. Square across from G.

 This line is needed for the front shoulder.

Back pattern lines

AH = one-sixth of the across back width.

AI = $\frac{1}{2}''$. Curve in the back neck from H to I.

FJ = half the across back width. Square a line from J up to the AC line. K is the centre of this line and $\frac{1}{4}''$ to the right. Join K to H for the shoulder.

EL = a quarter of the bust. Curve the armhole from L, through J to K.

Square a construction line from L down to M.

Front pattern lines

CH^2 = AH plus $\frac{1}{2}''$.

CI^2 = AH plus $1''$. Curve the front neck fairly deeply from H^2 to I^2.

H^2K^2 = HK. (K lies on the G construction line.)

F^2J^2 = half the across front width.

E^2L = a quarter of the bust plus $1''$. Curve the armhole, deeply, from L through J^2 to K^2.

Extend D to N for $1\frac{1}{2}''$ as the bust takes this amount up at the centre front. Square a construction line from N across to the LM line.

ON = a third of MD.

BP = $3''$ to $3\frac{1}{2}''$ as desired.

To make the waist fit, find the difference between half the bust and half the waist measurements. Take one third of this difference out to the right of P and another third out to the left of O in darts 5″ long. The remaining third is taken out equally either side of M as in the diagram, making the side seams. Draw in the front waist as shown.

CHILDREN'S BODICE PATTERNS are made in the same way with the following differences:
1) AE = two-thirds of AB.
2) Raise the back shoulder on to the G line.
3) DN = $\frac{1}{2}$″.
4) Take up $\frac{1}{2}$″ only in each dart.

Sleeve Block

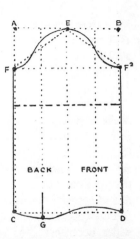

Measurements needed:
1) Round the arm (biceps).
2) Outside length.

Construction lines
Draw a rectangle ABCD.
AB = round the arm measurement.
AC = outside length.
Divide the rectangle into four, lengthwise.
E is the centre of AB.
AF = 5″ (Usual depth of sleevehead).
Join F to E and E to F².

Pattern lines
Curve the sleevehead, as in the diagram, making the curve below the EF line $\frac{1}{4}$″ deep and the one above it $\frac{3}{4}$″ deep. The curves above and below the EF² line are each $\frac{1}{2}$″ deep. Note where the curve crosses the line in each case. Keep it flat across the top at E.

Curve the wrist from C to D as shown, dipping the back $\frac{1}{2}$″ at G and raising the front $\frac{1}{4}$″ above the CD line.

G is the position of the wrist opening on the back quarter, 3″ long.

For a short sleeve cut across the pattern 5″, or less, below the FF² line, as indicated by the dot and dash line.

Measure the sleevehead and compare it with the armhole. It should be 1″ to 1$\frac{1}{2}$″ larger than the armhole and no more. This allows for easing over the shoulder.

CHILD'S SLEEVE BLOCK

AC = outside length plus $\frac{1}{2}''$.

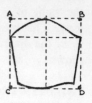

AB is the actual armhole measurement taken from the bodice block. Make a rectangle and divide it in half. Rule a line across below AB for the depth of the sleevehead, which is the difference between the outside and the inside arm lengths. (The inside arm length is taken straight down from the armpit to the wrist.) Curve the sleevehead as in the diagram. Curve the wrist from points $\frac{1}{2}''$ up and 1" in from C and D. Join the wrist to the armpit at each side.

Skirt Block Pattern

Measurements needed are:

1) The waist.
2) The hips.
3) The length.

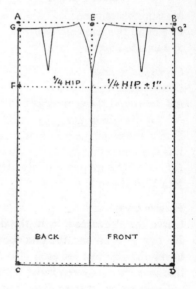

Construction lines
Make a rectangle ABCD. AB = half the hip plus 1" and AC = the length.

AF = 8". Square across from F for the hip line.

AE = a quarter of the hips.

 This makes the front pattern 1" wider because the body is wider across the front.

Pattern lines
Take $1\frac{1}{2}''$ out at either side of E and curve the side seams from these points to the hip line and then continue straight down to the hem. The distance in from the centre front and back of the waist darts is taken from the bodice block as they must match. They are 6" long and the amount taken out in each is half the difference between AB less 3" (the amount taken out at the side seams), and half the waist measurement. AG and BG² are both $\frac{1}{2}''$.

Curve in the waist lines.

Knicker Pattern

Measurements needed are:
1) The hips.
2) The crotch depth.

Construction lines

These are drafted exactly as for the skirt block but make AC = the depth of the crotch plus 5".

GH = the depth of the crotch plus 1" below AB. Extend each end of this line for one eighth of the hip measure for the fork points.

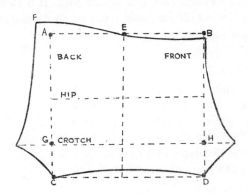

Pattern lines

F is one sixteenth of the hip measure to the right of A and $1\frac{1}{2}$" up. For the waist, curve from F through E to a point $\frac{1}{2}$" below B on the centre front line. The back waist is raised in this way to give extra depth to make the garment comfortable when sitting.

Curve the centre front and back seams from the waist to the fork points as in the diagram.

Curve the inside leg seams from the fork points to C and D.

The hem of the leg is curved from C to D raising it 1" on the E line.

For children, raise the back waist 1" higher, and curve the centre back seam slightly outwards instead of inwards and keep the centre front seam quite straight.

c

Block or foundation patterns are often used for making the paper patterns one buys in the shops. Any simple trade pattern which is a good fit may be used as an individual block pattern if the turnings are cut off, and may be adapted to many different styles. With a good sense of proportion and a little practice one can do this quite easily oneself.

Altering the Style of a Trade Pattern

Sometimes it is desirable to change some feature of a trade pattern by altering the type of collar or by adding fullness or a yoke and so on. The following examples show how this can be done. It is more easily done if the turnings are cut off the pattern, but on no account forget to allow them again when cutting out in the material.

REVERS COLLAR

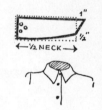

Measure the neck on the front and back pattern pieces. This gives the half neck measurement. Draw a rectangle 2½″ deep by the half neck measurement. Draw the collar as in the diagram, raising the neck edge ½″ at the front and extending the point 1″ or more.

PETER PAN COLLAR

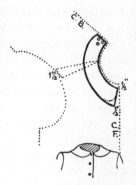

Place the back and the front shoulders of the pattern together overlapping them 1½″ at the shoulder end only. This tightens the outer edge and makes the collar stand up slightly. Pencil round the outline on a piece of paper. Draw the collar as in the diagram making it 2″–2½″ deep or more as desired. Drop the neck ½″ at the CF and take the point ½″ in from the CF. The front ends of the collar may be curved as in the dot and dash line.

PINAFORE TOP WITH SQUARE NECK AND FACING

1) Pencil round the front and back bodice patterns.

2) Draw the square neck as deep as is required.

3) Reduce the width of the shoulder equally on the back and the front.

4) Lower the armhole $1''$–$1\frac{1}{2}''$ on both back and front.

5) Cut out the new pattern and pencil round it on another piece of paper for the facing, the shape of which is shown by the dotted line.

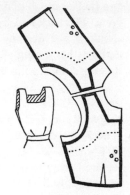

ADDING FULLNESS AND A YOKE

1) Place the back and front shoulders together and pencil round them on a piece of paper. Draw in the yoke There is now no shoulder seam.

2) Cut the pattern out.

3) For the back fullness cut the back pattern in half from the waist to the yoke end. Paste a strip of paper in the cut to give the desired amount of fullness.

4) In this style the front has fullness at the shoulder only and not at the waist. Cut the pattern through from the yoke end almost to the waist. Spread the required amount at the yoke end and paste paper behind.

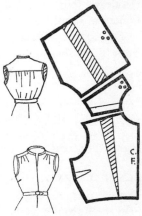

MAGYAR OR KIMONO SLEEVE

This type of sleeve is cut all in one piece with the bodice.

1) Place the back and front bodice pattern pieces on a piece of paper with the shoulders together. Keep the shoulders together at the neck but separate them $\frac{1}{2}''$ at the armhole end. Pencil round the outline.

2) Place the sleeve to the armhole as shown by the dotted line and pencil round.

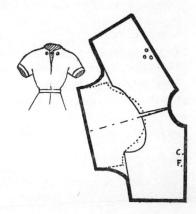

3) Curve the underarm seams and pencil round so that the sleeve and bodice are all in one piece.

Note. The back and front may be cut in two pieces with a seam at the shoulder, see dot and dash line. This is usually the case when the garment has a long sleeve because the width of the material prevents it being cut out all in one piece.

CAP SLEEVE

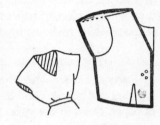

1) Pencil round the pattern and draw the V neck as indicated.

2) For the sleeve extend the shoulder the required length and curve the shoulder seam slightly from the neck to the end of the sleeve. Join the end of the sleeve to the underarm seam.

The back is altered in the same way but without altering the neck.

SHORT SLEEVE WITH FULL CROWN

Cut the pattern through the centre from the crown almost to the hem.

Spread the pattern at the crown to give the required fullness and paste paper behind.

PLAIN SLEEVE GATHERED INTO ARMBAND

Cut the pattern through the centre from the hem almost to the crown.

Spread at the hem and paste paper behind.

PUFF SLEEVE

Cut the pattern through the centre from the hem to the crown, and spread equally at both places. Paste paper behind. Lower the hem by 1″ in the centre and curve it so that the sleeve will pouch over the armband. The crown is also raised slightly in the centre.

CUFF

Pencil round the sleeve and raise the hem 1″ in the centre. Draw the cuff in as in the diagram making it the required depth. Alternative cuff shown by dotted line.

FLARED SKIRT

To make a straight skirt flared cut the pattern through from the hem almost to the waist.

Spread the pattern at the hem to give the desired amount of flare and paste paper behind.

Note. If the skirt is to be made very flared, almost circular, the pattern will have to be cut up in several places and spread out equally. Make sure that the waist is not reduced.

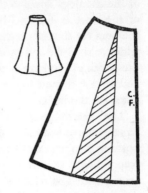
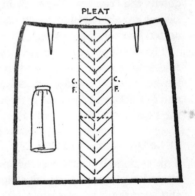

SKIRT WITH CENTRAL PLEAT

Pencil round the pattern and add twice the depth of the pleat on to the centre front, that is for a pleat 2″ deep add 4″. Reverse the pattern and pencil round it again.

If the material is bulky the top of the part inserted for the pleat may be cut away down to the line dotted across. If this part is cut away do not forget to allow turnings.

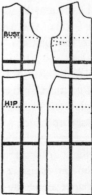

Altering the Size of a Trade Pattern

Patterns for garments with a bodice, such as blouses, dresses, petticoats and so on, are chosen by the *BUST* measure and those for skirts, slacks and knickers by the *HIP* measure, even though the other measurements may not all be correct. When some of the measurements differ from those of the individual, and few people conform entirely to the standard, the pattern must be altered to fit. This is done before cutting out to avoid wasting material. Pin the parts of the pattern together and fit it on the wearer. Adjustments can then be made at the places indicated on the diagrams.

The length of the bodice is altered *BELOW* the bust line and the width through the centre of the shoulder down to the waist. The length of the skirt is adjusted between the hip and the hem for the reason that the hem is usually wider at the base and by altering it in this way the width of the hem is not reduced as would be the case if the extra length was taken off the hem.

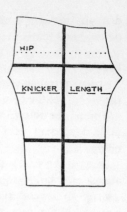

The sleeve length is altered equally above and below the elbow position, as the arm should be correspondingly shorter or longer in each place. The width is changed down the centre. Tight fitting

sleeves are altered in the same place and the shape of it is shown by the dotted lines on the diagram.

The depth between the waist and the crotch on knicker type garments is altered between the hip and the crotch. The leg length in knickers and shorts is adjusted at the hem and in slacks and pyjamas, between the crotch and the hem.

ENLARGING A PATTERN

This is done by cutting across the pattern at the alteration places and pasting strips of paper in the slits to make it the necessary size.

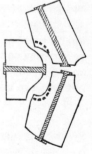

If the sleeve is widened the original armhole will be too small and must be enlarged by cutting away a little of the pattern as shown by the dotted lines in the diagram.

REDUCING A PATTERN

Pin tucks across the pattern at the alteration places. For instance if a bodice is 1″ too long take up a tuck ½″ deep and this will reduce the pattern by the required amount. This entails a slight adjustment on the side seam which will no longer run in a straight line. Paste a piece of paper along the side to make it straight.

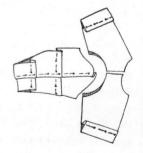

If the sleeve is taken in, the armhole must be correspondingly reduced by adding paper to the underarm as shown by the shaded portion in the diagram.

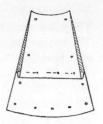

When a flared skirt is shortened the side seam is again thrown out and must be straightened by pasting paper along the side.

The waist of a dress may be reduced by taking in the side seam, or by introducing a dart, or by enlarging one already there. It may be enlarged by letting out a dart or by adding to the side seam. Remember that if the waist of the bodice is altered the skirt must be altered also to match.

Perforations and Markings on Paper Patterns

There are two types of paper pattern (1) those which have instructions and lines printed on them and (2) those which are perforated with various sized holes. Patterns are cut to the standard measurements and turnings are allowed *outside* these measurements. Some patterns have $\frac{5}{8}''$ and others $\frac{1}{2}''$ turnings allowed. The depth of the turnings is indicated on the pattern by a printed line or by small perforated holes. *This is the fitting line and it is of the utmost importance.* It is, as its name implies, the line on which the garment fits. If the seams are stitched up outside this line the garment becomes too large and if they are stitched inside too small.

Unless a style is not symmetrical only half the pattern is given, and when cutting out, some parts of the pattern may have to be placed to a fold in the material so that when opened out they are in one piece. When a part has to be so placed it may be shown on a pattern by three holes placed together to form a triangle, by two medium holes placed immediately under each other, by a short slit or it may have 'place to a fold' printed on it, depending on the make of pattern.

The positions of darts, pockets and buttonholes are marked with small holes but the latter are sometimes marked with square perforations.

Large holes punched at intervals immediately under each other indicate the grain line and must all be placed on a straight thread of the material. This is very important to the fit and hang of any garment.

Balance marks

These are small notches printed or cut out of the edges of the pattern.
The notches on one piece of pattern will match those on another piece
and show that the two pieces are to be joined together.

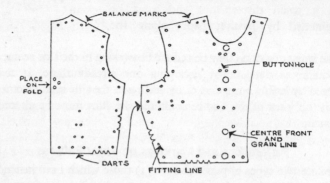

When using a trade pattern it is helpful to pencil in the outlines by
connecting the perforations. This gives a clearer idea of the shapes of
the pattern pieces.

IV: The Sequence
of Making Up a Garment

Before cutting out, the material may have to be treated to prevent the possibility of it shrinking when the garment is washed or cleaned. Woollen materials must be damp-pressed (this is explained in the chapter on pressing). Unless guaranteed pre-shrunk, cottons are very liable to shrink and they are best wrapped in a wet sheet or cloth until they are thoroughly damp, preferably overnight, and then ironed dry.

Assuming that the pattern has been pinned together, tried on, and adjusted to fit, the general rules for laying the pattern on the material are as follows:

1) If the material is to be folded in half lengthwise, see that the selvedge edges are exactly together. Some inexpensive cottons are rolled badly during manufacture and the threads become pulled slightly out of the true direction so that when the selvedges are together the torn ends are not level. When this happens, two people should each hold one end and pull the material sharply diagonally until the ends become level.

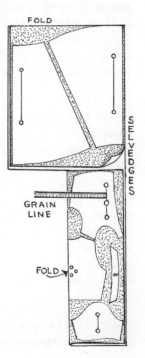

2) Study the material for nap. If there is a pile or one way pattern, all the pattern pieces must be placed the right way up. If there is no nap, pattern pieces may be turned upside down, should they fit in more economically this way.

3) If the material has stripes or checks, make certain that these will match at the seams.

4) Pencil the grain line in on the pattern and make sure it lies on a straight thread of the material. Measure in from the selvedge for accuracy. Unless this is done the garment will not hang correctly nor wear well.

5) Lay all the large pieces first and then, if possible, fit the smaller pieces into the spaces left.

6) Look for the perforations denoting that pieces are placed on the fold of the material and place these edges absolutely on the fold, for if they are placed only $\frac{1}{4}''$ inside the fold the garment will be $\frac{1}{2}''$ too large as the material is double.

7) If pattern pieces have to be cut out singly, to avoid wasting material, remember to reverse the pattern when cutting for the second time, so that left and right sides are cut. If the pattern is not symmetrical, that is the left and right sides are differ-

ent, the pattern pieces must be placed the right way up on the right side of the material in order that they may be cut for the correct sides.

8) Pin the pattern pieces firmly to the material, pinning across the corners and then about every $4''$–$6''$ between. Keep the pattern and material *FLAT* on the table when putting in the pins. See diagram.

9) If no turnings are allowed on the pattern they must be chalked on to the material before cutting out.

10) Lay *ALL* the pattern pieces on the material before cutting out any of them to make sure that they will all fit into the material.

Cutting Out

1) Cut the material with long sweeping cuts to avoid jagging the edges. If turnings are allowed, cut close to the pattern edge.

2) Cut all balance marks *OUTWARDS*. This is important, for if they are cut inwards the seams cannot be let out during fitting and the edges are difficult to neaten. If the pattern pieces are arranged so closely together that the balance marks cannot be cut out-

BALANCE MARKS CUT OUTWARDS

wards, cut straight across them and mark them in later with tailor tacks.

3) During cutting keep the material and scissors touching the table. On no account lift the material, tempting as it may be to do so.

Taking Out and Tacking Up

When all the pieces have been cut out, proceed as follows:

1) All the fitting lines must be marked out on the material, with tailor

tacks for woollen and cotton materials, and by tracing out with flat
tacking for silks and nylons. (See Temporary Stitches, page 37.) This
MUST be carried out with the work *FLAT* on the table and not raised
in any way.

2) After tracing, remove the pattern pieces and wrap them up with
the pieces of material for future identification.

3) Any tucking or gathering should be
done first. When a flat piece is to be joined
to a gathered piece, make two rows of fine
running stitches ⅛" apart, one row just below
the fitting line and the other just above
it. Pull these threads up to gather to the
required size. Pin the fitting lines of the two
pieces together on the gathered side, placing
the pins vertically so that the gathers may be
more easily regulated. Tack and stitch
through the fitting lines. This makes the join
lie between the gathering rows. The lower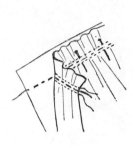
row will show on the right side and may be removed if desired, after
machining.

4) Pin and tack up the darts from the wide end towards the point.

5) Pin all the seams of the bodice, sleeves and skirt together matching
the fitting lines everywhere. Pin *ACROSS* the seams as this prevents
the top piece of material slipping along on the
under piece.

6) Tack the seams through the fitting lines
keeping the work flat on the table.

7) Tack the sleeves into the armholes according to the type. For the methods refer to the
chapter on sleeves.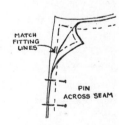

8) Tack patch pockets in position.

9) To join the bodice to the skirt, mark the
centre fronts and backs with pins. Keep the
skirt wrong side out, then turn the bodice
right side out and slip it inside the skirt,
bringing the waist seams together. Pin the
centre backs and fronts together and the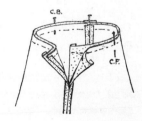
side seams, and then pin between. Tack
the fitting lines together. The garment is now
ready for fitting.

Fitting
Try the garment on and fit the right hand side only, unless the figure is not the same both sides, when each side will have to be fitted separately.

POINTS TO LOOK FOR WHEN FITTING

1) Sloping shoulders require the shoulder seam to be taken up at the outer end as in the diagram. This will reduce the armhole which may have to be lowered under the arm to make the sleeve fit.

2) For square shoulders let the seam out a little on the outer end.

3) Sometimes the back neck is loose if people are round shouldered. Take the fullness away in two small darts.

4) The shoulders may be too long. Place pins to show where the sleeves are to be set in.

5) Sleeves should hang slightly forward with the grain of the material running from the top of the shoulder to the little finger, and straight across the armhole. If they hang badly, untack and move round in the armhole until the correct position is obtained. Remember that the sleeve seam should never lie behind the side seam of the bodice.

6) If the garment is too large at the waist, reduce it by taking in the side seams and by increasing the depth of the darts on *both* the bodice and the skirt.

7) If the waist is too low, tie a tape round the natural waist and pin in the correct position on the bodice.

8) Should the skirt be tight across the hips, lift it up at the waist, but bear in mind that this will shorten it and may leave very little allowance for the hem.

TRANSFERRING THE CORRECTIONS TO THE OTHER SIDE

Replace the correcting pins with coloured tacking to denote the new fitting line clearly.

Fold the right hand side of the garment accurately over the left hand side and pin through the alteration lines. Transfer the new fitting lines to the other side with tacking.

**The Order of
Making Up**

Take the sleeves out and untack the bodice from the skirt, then proceed to make up as follows:
1) Attach or make any pockets.
2) Stitch all the darts and the seams and neaten them where necessary. Press well.
3) If there are facings to a button through front, attach them.
4) Make up the collar, cuffs and belt.
5) Attach the collar to the bodice. Occasionally this is more easily done before the side seams of the bodice are stitched up.
6) Make buttonholes, if any, on the bodice. If the garment buttons from the neck to the hem, the buttonholes cannot be worked until after the waist seam is joined.
7) Finish the ends of the sleeves, i.e. make wrist openings, hems or attach cuffs.
8) Insert the sleeves and neaten seam. *Note.* If sleeves are of the raglan or shirt blouse types, they are attached to the bodice before the side seams are stitched. See chapter on sleeves for the methods.
9) Join the bodice to the skirt. Press the seam open, or up on to the bodice, as is most convenient, and neaten.
10) Work the side opening.
11) Fit on the wearer and level and finish the hem.
12) Give a final pressing.
13) Sew on buttons, press studs and hooks and eyes.

   Note. If the bodice, the skirt and the sleeves are made up and finished as far as possible, before joining them together, they are more easily handled.

THE DIRECTION IN WHICH SEAMS SHOULD BE STITCHED

Shoulder seams From the neck towards the armhole.

Bodice side seams From the armhole to the waist.

Darts Begin at the wide end and taper evenly and gradually to the narrow end. The last four stitches should lie actually on the fold.

Sleeve seams From the armpit to the wrist.

Skirt seams From the hem to the waist.

V: Temporary, Permanent and Decorative Stitches

Temporary Stitches

Temporary stitches are used to transfer the fitting lines from patterns on to material, for tacking parts together prior to stitching, as a guide for machining and for holding parts, such as pleats and revers, temporarily in position. Eventually they are entirely removed. Their importance cannot be over estimated and they should never be scamped, for in the long run much time is saved.

TAILOR TACKING

Used to transfer fitting lines to woollen and cotton materials. Choose a needle which can be threaded easily and thread it with long double tacking cotton. (Always use tacking cotton as it is fluffy and stays in the material as other cottons do not.)

Method 1. For use with patterns where the fitting lines are marked with per- forations. Take a small stitch through a hole in the pattern and through both layers of material. Take a stitch back in the same hole and pull the cotton through leaving a loop $\frac{1}{4}''-\frac{1}{2}''$ deep. Pass on to the next hole and repeat. Cut the threads between each hole. When all the holes have been tailor tacked, remove the pins and lift the pattern off. Pull the two layers of material apart gently, and cut through the stitches between them, leaving half the threads in each piece of

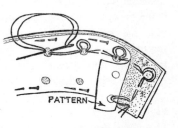

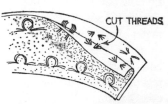

material. Mark buttonholes, pocket positions, darts and balance marks with different coloured cottons so that they may be recognized easily.

Method 2. For use with patterns with printed fitting lines. Tack through the pattern and the material with stitches $\frac{1}{2}''$ long and leave

loops 1ʳ deep between each stitch.
Cut through each loop and remove
the pattern. Part the material very
carefully, for there is now no loop to
prevent the cotton pulling completely
through. Cut the threads between as
before.

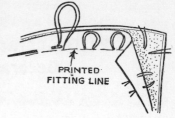

PRINTED
FITTING LINE

Use this method also, for marking
round the outside edges of patterns which have no turnings allowed
but, in this case, there is no need to cut the loops; just separate the
material and cut between.

TRACING OUT

A more secure method for marking the
fitting lines on slippery materials, such as
nylons, rayons and silks, when tailor tacks
would fall out.

Method. Pin the pattern and the material
through the fitting lines, then turn to the
underside and, parting the two layers of
material with a finger, tack through the top
layer only, connecting the pins. When this
side has been tacked, pin both layers of
material together through the tacking lines;
turn over and remove the pattern. Then
trace the other side in the same way.

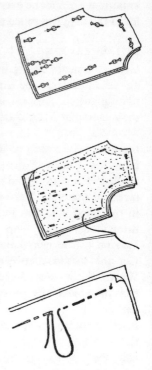

FLAT TACKING

Used for tracing out, as above, and for
holding parts together ready for stitching.

Method. Begin with a knot, pass over ½" of
material and take up a stitch ⅛" long. Continue in this way, making alternate long
and short stitches, which hold the work
together more securely than stitches of an
even length.

SLIP TACKING

Very useful for tacking together curved edges and seams where stripes
and checks have to match, as it is worked on the right side of the garment.

Method. Fold under the turnings on one piece of material and lap it over those of the other piece making the fitting lines match. Pin securely across the seam. Take *SMALL* stitches, alternately, through the fitting line of the flat piece and then through the *FOLD* only, of the turning which was folded under, as indicated in the diagram. When the pins are removed, it will be seen that the seam is tacked, as normally, on the wrong side and is ready for stitching.

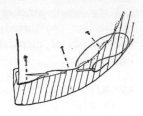

STRAIGHT TACKING
Used as a guide for machining.
Method. Begin with a knot and a stitch, then, with the left hand, pull the cotton straight along the required position of the machining and hold it firmly. Tack along the line of cotton, taking up only a few threads of material between each stitch.

BASTING
Used to hold pleats and revers in position until the garment is completed.
Method. Put the needle upright into the material and pull through. Repeat a little further along making slanting stitches as in the diagram.

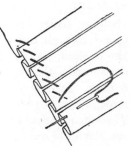

Permanent Stitches
Permanent stitches are those which hold parts of a garment together and they may be made by hand or by machine.

RUNNING
Used for stitching seams and for gathering.
Method. To begin, take a small stitch through the material, see A. Then take a backstitch over it keeping the thread under the needle point, see B. This will hold

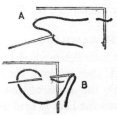

D

the thread.

Make small stitches by passing the needle over two threads and then under two threads of material. End off as for beginning on.

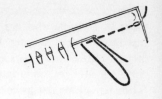

RUNNING AND AN OCCASIONAL BACK-STITCH

This is a little stronger than just running. *Method.* Make three running stitches and then take one stitch back over the last space. Repeat.

BACKSTITCH

Used to hold parts together very firmly and to imitate machine stitching. Make a running stitch and a space, then take the needle back over the space and bring it out the length of the stitch in front of the hanging thread.

HEMMING

Used for fixing hems. To begin, run the needle through the fold of the hem from left to right, see A. Tuck the end of the thread under the edge of the hem and hold it there. Take very small, slanting stitches through the material and the hem, see B. The stitches should show on the right side and should be very even and close together. To end off, make two over stitches and slip the needle along inside the hem for about 1″, then bring it out through the hem and cut the thread, see C.

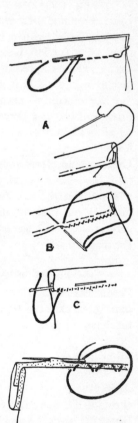

SLIP HEMMING

An invisible method for the hems of dresses and skirts. Fold the garment over level with the edge of the hem. To work the stitch the hem is held away from the worker.

Begin on as for hemming. Pick up one thread of the garment and $\frac{1}{8}''$ further along, slip the needle through the edge of the hem for $\frac{1}{4}''$. Pull the thread through, not too tightly, and repeat.

HERRINGBONE STITCH

Used for seams in flannel garments, hems in thick material and as an embroidery stitch.

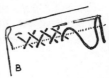

The stitch is worked from the left to the right. Begin by making a small backstitch as at A. Put the needle into the work $\frac{1}{4}''$ along below the hem from the right to the left, taking up a stitch $\frac{1}{8}''$ long. Take the needle up $\frac{1}{4}''$ further along level with the beginning on stitch, and take another stitch $\frac{1}{8}''$ long from the right to the left. The stitch crosses each time. End off with a back stitch, see C.

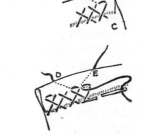

To join the thread, finish the old thread with an upward stitch bringing the needle out at the beginning of the stitch before, then make a backstitch, see D. The new thread is brought through the hem $\frac{1}{8}''$ to the left of the last upward stitch, see E. Make a backstitch and then continue to herringbone.

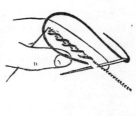

OVERSEWING

This is a means of neatening a raw seam edge.

Always work against the grain of the material, tying it down. Hold the work along the first finger of the left hand. Begin with a few running stitches from the right to the left, then make slanting stitches $\frac{1}{8}''$ apart and $\frac{1}{8}''$ deep over the raw edge. The stitches must lie level with the edge and not be pulled tight in any way.

WHIPPING

Used to finish a raw edge and to attach lace. Roll the edge tightly between finger and thumb to the wrong side of the garment.

With the wrong side towards the worker make small stitches over the rolled edge and pull them tight.

BLANKET STITCH OR LOOP STITCH

Used to neaten a raw edge and as an embroidery stitch. Begin with a few running stitches in the reverse direction. Put the needle in $\frac{1}{8}''$ from the raw edge. Hold the thread under the point of the needle forming a loop on the edge. Pull the needle through, see diagram. End off by running a few stitches back into the edge of the material.

BUTTONHOLE STITCH

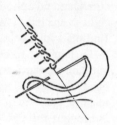

Used for buttonholes and for sewing on fasteners. Put the needle into the material behind the raw edge, bringing it out $\frac{1}{8}''$ inside the edge. Take the thread where it enters the eye of the needle and twist it round the point as in the diagram. Pull the needle through and up, bringing the knot on the raw edge and, at the same time, pinching the stitch between finger and thumb to make it even.

SEAMING

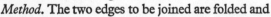

Used for attaching patches and patch pockets as invisibly as possible by hand, and also for sewing lace to a finished edge.
Method. The two edges to be joined are folded and held together as in the diagram. To begin, tuck the end of the thread between the edges and bring the needle out through one edge. Working from the left to the right, make small oversewing stitches taking up one thread only of the material from each edge. The stitches must be very close so that they do not show when the work is opened out flat.

FISHBONE STITCH

Used to hold two raw edges together prior to darning.
Method. To begin, run the cotton through the material for a short distance. Bring the needle up on the right side and insert it in the slit and

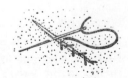

under the raw edge of one side. Bring it out ⅛″ in from the edge, or more if the material frays. A little higher up insert the needle under the opposite edge. Repeat this drawing the edges together.

STAB STITCH

Used for holding the bindings of pockets and buttonholes in position and for inserting zip fasteners. It is also used for saddle stitching as a decorative edge, and for quilting.

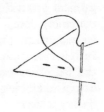

Method. Make small stitches passing the needle down and up through the material in an upright position.

TAILOR'S CATCH

Used to reinforce weak places, such as the ends of pockets and the tops of pleats.

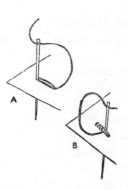

Method. Make three stab stitches over each other ₃⁄₁₆″ long, see A. Work over this bar with tiny stab stitches until it is completely covered, as at B.

ARROWHEADS

A more decorative way of strengthening the ends of pockets and the tops of pleats.

Method. Cut a paper shape and outline it with tacking on the material. This helps to keep the sides straight and is useful for keeping a uniform size when more than one arrowhead is worked on a garment.

Begin with a backstitch on the wrong side and bring the needle to the right side through the bottom left hand corner. Take a tiny stitch from the right to the left through the top of the triangle.

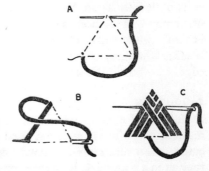

Put the needle in the bottom right hand corner and bring it out just inside the stitch on the left hand side.

Continue in this way making each stitch at the top a little wider and a fraction lower than the one above and each stitch at the bottom, just inside the previous one. Work until the triangle is filled with stitching.

Decorative Stitches

There are two kinds of decoration. One type merely beautifies a garment or article and serves no other purpose. Examples of this are the embroidering of corners on tablecloths and the working of initials on underwear. The other kind is functional as well as being decorative. In this case satin stitch may be a means of attaching lace to an edge and faggotting can be used as a method of adding a false hem. The latter is the better type and the former is often only a disguise for poor quality material.

HEMSTITCHING

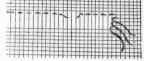

Can be used to fasten a hem on household articles or it may be used as pure decoration on garments.

Method. The first thread to be drawn from the material is cut through 1″ short at each end, and is drawn out carefully. With the help of a needle the 1″ at each end is drawn back to the required position. This prevents the possibility of overcutting the corners and the hanging ends may be trimmed off afterwards. Draw out the desired number of threads in this way.

To begin, run a few stitches through the material in a reverse direction. Work from the right side and pass the needle behind four threads of the material from the right to the left, and pull through. Put the needle down into the hem for a depth of two threads as in the diagram. Make sure that the hem is caught in, behind, with each down stitch. Blanket stitch any corners. The top edge is worked in the same way.

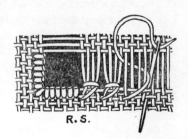

R. S.

FAGGOTING

A decorative method of joining two pieces of material together. It is often used for making entire collars and cuffs by connecting lengths of rouleau in a pattern. It is a very good way to apply a false hem.

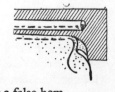

Method. Fold under the raw edges of the turnings to the fitting line. Tack the material right side up, on to strong paper. The tacking stitches must be small and only $\frac{1}{16}$" in from the edge of the material. The distance apart of the two edges to be joined, should be $\frac{3}{16}$". The stitch is worked with fine silk or buttonhole twist, from the right to the left.

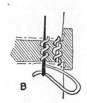

A

LADDER FAGGOTING

1) Begin with a knot slipped between the folded edge. Bring the needle out through the top edge and insert it in the lower edge from underneath, see A.

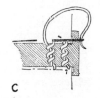

B

2) Twist the point of the needle three times round the bar thus formed, and pull the thread through, see B.

3) Slip the needle along in the top fold for $\frac{1}{8}$" and repeat from the beginning, see C.

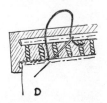

C

4) When the stitches have been worked, press the work while still attached to the paper and oversew the unfinished edges finely between the faggoting stitches, see D. Remove the paper.

5) On the wrong side trim all raw edges to $\frac{1}{8}$" and whip them over tightly and closely to neaten.

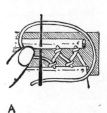

D

FANCY FAGGOTING

1) Begin as before and bring the needle up in the lower edge.

2) Put the needle into the top edge from underneath $\frac{1}{8}$" further along, with the thread under the point as in the illustration at A. Pull the thread through and *DOWNWARDS*. This is important to get the twist in the stitch.

A

3) Insert the needle $\frac{1}{8}$" further along under the lower edge, keeping the thread under the point.

Pull through and *UPWARDS*, see B. Repeat from the beginning.

To join the thread in the middle of the work, make an upward stitch without putting the thread under the point, then run the thread a short way along the fold and back and cut it off. Run the new thread through the fold bringing it out at the last stitch. Put the needle behind the upright bar from the left to the right and pull through. This will form the twist.

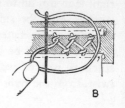

PUNCH STITCHES

These stitches, like faggoting, resemble drawn thread work and may be used for fastening hems, for making seams and for attaching lace to raw edges. They are useful for filling in backgrounds in embroidery designs. All these stitches must be worked with a thick needle and be pulled tight to form the holes. The diagrams are self explanatory.

PUNCH STITCH

Follow the diagram from the right to the left. Pull each stitch tight to separate the threads of the material and form the holes.

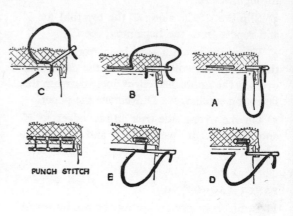

PUNCH STITCH

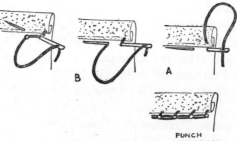

PUNCH
HEMSTITCH

PIN STITCH

A three sided version of punch stitch. Follow the diagram from the right to the left.

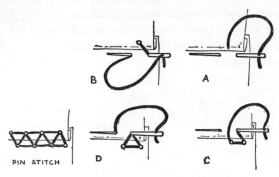

PIN STITCH   B   A   D   C

SATIN STITCH

Make over and over stitches through the material. For a raised effect the stitch may be worked over a cord.

STEM STITCH   SATIN STITCH

CROSS STITCH

This is best worked on material where the threads can be counted. Make slanting stitches by putting the needle upright into the material as in the diagram. Count the threads between each stitch, 3 to 6 according to the coarseness of the material. Work the stitches all one way first and then work back, crossing them.

CROSS STITCH

KNOTTED STITCHES

French knot

Make a small back stitch and then twist the thread twice round the needle point. Hold the threat taut and pull the needle through. Put the needle back into the material where the thread first came up and bring it out at the position of the next knot. Repeat.

FRENCH KNOT

A   KNOT STITCH

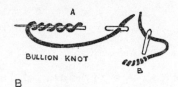

A

BULLION KNOT   B

B

CORAL STITCH

ZIGZAG CORAL

C

LOOP STITCHES

ZIGZAG FEATHER

LOOP STITCH
VARIATIONS

CHAIN STITCHES

CHAIN STITCH

D   CHEQUERED CHAIN

E   ZIGZAG CHAIN

FLY STITCH   F

LAZY DAISY

VI: Seams

The fit and outline of a garment depend very largely on the way in which the seams are made. Crooked seams give crooked outlines. It is extremely important to be accurate when tacking up seams and to pay great attention to the fitting line, for if seams are stitched outside it, the garment becomes too big, and if inside it, too small.

The type of seam to use depends on the thickness of the material and on the amount of wear and tear the garment will have to withstand. Children's clothes, shirts and overalls, for instance, receive hard wear and constant laundering and so need very strong seams, such as double stitched or French seams. Dresses and thicker materials need a much flatter seam, such as the plain seam, while flannel has seams all to itself, as it is used mainly for babies' clothes and French seams would be too bulky and would be too long drying when laundered.

The seams should be as inconspicuous as possible, except when they are deliberately stressed, as by piping or stitching for example, as a special feature of the garment. Press each seam as it is made and especially before joining it to another. When pressing it is important not to leave an impression of the seam on the right side.

Plain Seam

This is the flattest seam of all and is used for dresses, skirts, slacks, shorts, etc., in fact for most outer wear.

1) Place together the two pieces to be joined with the right sides inside and the fitting lines matching. Pin through at intervals, inserting the pins across the seam, as this prevents the top layer of material from shifting along on the under one. Tack on the fitting line. Remove the pins before machining unless the material has stripes or checks which have to be matched; in that case leave the pins in and take the machine needle over them very carefully. This prevents the presser foot of the machine from pushing the top along and disarranging the pattern.

2) Machine on the fitting line and right through the turnings at each end of the seam.

3) Remove the tacking and press the seam open flat on the wrong side.

TO NEATEN THE EDGES

There are various ways of neatening the edges depending on the type of material.

a) Oversewing. This is a suitable method for almost all types of material, except for those which fray badly. It is the flattest way of neatening the edge and is used for dresses, and most outer wear, particularly when made of woollen material.

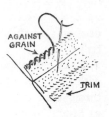

Trim the turnings to ½″ (¾″ to 1″ may be left on skirts). Oversew *AGAINST* the grain of the material tying it down. Oversewing with the grain will pull away.

b) Edge stitching. A strong finish which launders well. It is used on cotton, rayon and fine wool but is not suitable for heavier materials as it is more bulky than oversewing and when pressed is inclined to leave an impression on the right side. Decide on this method of finishing *BEFORE* cutting out and leave ¾″ turnings everywhere, for the pattern may have ½″ turnings only allowed. With the R.S. of the seam uppermost, turn the edge under with the point of the scissors, making the seam ½″ wide (a marker may be used to check the width) while machining quite on the folded edge. When machining the second side use the first side as a guide for the width. Trim away any surplus material close to the stitching.

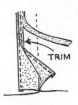

c) Blanket stitch. This is used for lingerie, blouses, material which frays and for all knitted fabrics. Trim the raw edges to ½″ and work blanket stitch over them, making the stitches ⅛″ deep and ⅛″ apart.

d) Binding. A useful finish for the seams of unlined dressing gowns and for skirts when the material frays badly and also for armholes and waist

seams when the two edges are neatened together. For the method see crossway binding under 'Finishing edges'. Paris binding may be used in place of crossway.

French Seam

This is a very strong seam which neatens itself. It is used extensively for children's wear, for lingerie and blouses. It can be used only on thin material as it is a little bulky.

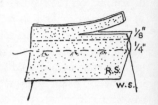

1) Place the pieces to be joined together with the right sides outside. Pin and tack through the fitting lines.

2) Stitch (by hand or machine) $\frac{1}{4}''$ outside the fitting line ($\frac{1}{8}''$ for narrow seams on very fine material).

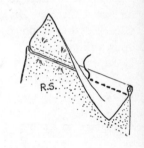

3) Remove the tacking. Trim the turnings to $\frac{1}{8}''$ or less for narrow seams, and press over to one side.

4) Turn the work to the W.S. and fold over on the seam line. Tack the fitting lines together again and stitch along them enclosing the raw edges completely.

5) Press the seam over towards the back of the garment unless, for any reason, it is more convenient for it to fall the other way. Lift the seam and press underneath it to avoid leaving an impression on the R.S.

Run and Fell Seam

This seam is used for garments which are worn next to the skin and for knickers, because it is flat and comfortable in wear.

1) Place the material together with the right sides inside. Pin and tack through the fitting lines.

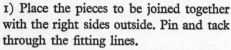

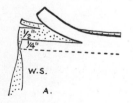

2) Run by hand along the fitting lines and remove the tacking.
3) Cut one turning to ¼″ and the other to ½″. Fold the edge of the wider turning over the narrow one to touch the running stitches.
4) Fold over again quite flat on to the garment. Tack and hem to position.

DOUBLE STITCHED SEAM

A variation of the run and fell which is stronger. The seam is machined instead of being made by hand see diagram (D). Diagram (E) is another way of making this seam and is used for shirts, some blouses, pyjamas and overalls.

1) Place the material together with the right sides *outside* and then proceed as for a run and fell seam, but machine it. This way both rows of machining show on the R.S.

Note. When trimming the turnings arrange for them to appear to fold over towards the back of the garment on the R.S.

Flannel Seams

These are used mostly for babies' wear as they are flat and comfortable.
a) Proceed as for a run and fell seam as far as trimming the turnings, making one ⅛″ and the other ¼″ wide. Fold the wider one flat over the narrow one and herringbone the raw edge to the garment.
b) This is just the plain seam with the turnings trimmed to ¼″ and herringboned to the garment.

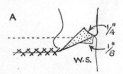

Overlaid or Top Stitched Seam

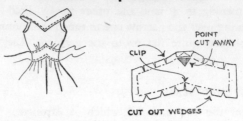

This strong seam is used when the shapes of the pieces to be joined make it difficult to use any of the preceding types of seam. The example given is a curved waist band inserted in a nightdress.

1) Clip the turnings across to the fitting line on the concave curve at the top of the band to enable them to turn over smoothly.

2) Fold the point over to the fitting line and cut it away leaving $\frac{1}{8}''$ turning only.

3) Cut wedge shaped snips out of the turnings on the lower convex curves, to prevent them rippling when turned over.

4) Tack the turnings over to the W.S. keeping a good line on the folded edge and tack.

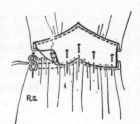

5) With the R.S. uppermost, pin the band into position over the gathered parts of the garment, matching the fitting lines. Place the pins vertically to keep the gathering uniform.

6) Tack and machine the edges of the band into position.

7) Trim the turnings and blanket stitch together.

STITCHING CROSSWAY TO STRAIGHT MATERIAL

Always stitch with the bias or crossway piece underneath and the material cut on the straight grain uppermost, as this prevents the crossway material from stretching.

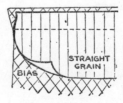

Thinning Seams

Flatness is always aimed at in needlework and sometimes when seams are bulky they may have to be trimmed down.

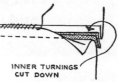

1) When four thicknesses are stitched together, as in a piped seam, trim the two inner turnings to $\frac{1}{8}''$. Trim the outer turnings to $\frac{1}{2}''$ and oversew them together.

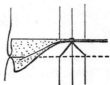

INNER TURNINGS
CUT DOWN

2) When two plain seams meet in a join, press them flat open before joining them together, and, after joining, trim the turnings beyond the stitching as shown in the diagram.

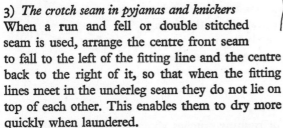

3) *The crotch seam in pyjamas and knickers*
When a run and fell or double stitched seam is used, arrange the centre front seam to fall to the left of the fitting line and the centre back to the right of it, so that when the fitting lines meet in the underleg seam they do not lie on top of each other. This enables them to dry more quickly when laundered.

When French seams are used turn them away from each other. French seams are not very satisfactory as they are a little bulky anyhow.

E

VII: Methods of Introducing and Disposing of Fullness

Fullness is introduced into garments in several ways, usually decoratively. The following methods show how this is done.

Gathering

Begin on with a very secure backstitch.

Make two rows of fine running stitches $\frac{1}{8}''$ apart, the top one just above the fitting line and the second just below it.

Pull both threads up together to the required size.

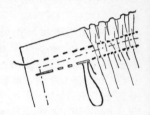

Shirring

Work several rows of running stitches about $\frac{1}{4}''$ apart. Pull them up together the required amount.

To prevent the threads from breaking in wear they are usually backed with a fine piece of material. Cut the material on the straight grain, fold the raw edges over all round and press. Pin and tack over the back of the shirring and hem to the garment.

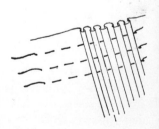

Gauging

This method can introduce a very great amount of material into a small width. Also it is used in the preparation of smocking.

Make rows of running stitches each stitch and each space being exactly under the one above. The length of the stitch and space depends on the amount of fullness required.

Smocking

Allow four times as much material as the desired finished width of smocking. That is, one yard of material will draw up into 9″ of smocking.

This varies a little with the size of the smocking paper. Dots spaced widely apart take up more material.

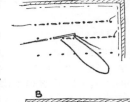

1) Tack the smocking paper to the W.S. of the material.

2) Using strong cotton of a different colour begin with a large knot and pick up two threads of material through each dot as at A. Leave the cotton hanging at the end of the row. Alternatively put the needle in at one dot and out at the next as at B.

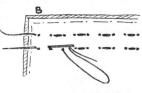

3) When all the rows have been worked tear away the paper very carefully beginning from the knot end.

4) Pull all the threads up together tightly to set the pleats. Then loosen them to two thirds of the finished width. Tie them off, two and two, with reef knots.

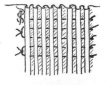

Beginning on for smocking

1) On the W.S. take a stitch in the second right hand pleat.

2) Make an over stitch to secure the thread. Push the needle between the first and second pleats through to the R.S.

Fasten off in the same way by pushing the needle between the last and last but one pleat and making one or two overstitches on the W.S.

The stitches may be worked with any embroidery cottons or silks.

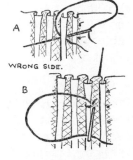

WRONG SIDE.

STEM STITCH

Put the needle into each pleat separately, from the right to the left holding the thread below the needle all the time. Pull the needle through and tighten the stitch.

If the gathering thread is of a different colour
from the material, it acts as a guide for keeping
the stitching straight.

CABLE STITCH

Work this as for stem stitch but hold the thread
alternately above and below the needle.

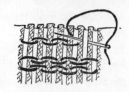

DOUBLE CABLE

Work a second row of single cable immediately
under the first row, touching it. Where the
thread was held above the needle in the first
row it must be held below it in the second row to make the stitches
alternate.

TRELLIS STITCH

1) Bring the thread up in the first pleat on
the left hand side, and holding it below the
needle, take a stitch level in the next pleat.
2) Keeping the thread below the needle,
take one stitch in each of the next two
pleats, each stitch a little higher than the
one before.
3) With the thread above the needle, take
one stitch level in the next pleat and then
one down in each of the next two pleats.
Repeat from 1.

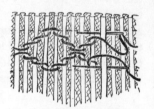

VANDYKE STITCH

Worked from the right to the left.
1) Take the 1st and 2nd pleats together
and take one stitch over them.
2) On the gathering thread below, take the
2nd and 3rd pleats together and then take another stitch over them.
3) Go up to the 1st gathering thread again and take the 3rd and 4th
pleats together and one over them. Continue in
this way.

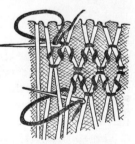

FEATHER STITCH

Work from right to left, and hold the work

sideways. Work ordinary feather stitch (see decorative stitches), taking one stitch in each pleat.

HONEYCOMB

This is more elastic and takes up only twice as much material as the finished width and is used when less fullness is needed.

1) Come up in the 1st pleat on the left side. Take a stitch over the 1st and 2nd pleats.

2) Pass the needle up inside the second pleat to the gathering row above.

3) Take the 2nd and 3rd pleats together and pass the needle down inside the 3rd pleat to the lower gathering thread. Continue in this way.

SURFACE HONEYCOMB

1) Come up in the 1st pleat and with the thread above the needle, take a stitch level in the 2nd pleat. In the same pleat take a stitch on the gathering row below. Take a level stitch in the 3rd pleat and then another one in the same pleat on the gathering row above. Repeat from 1.

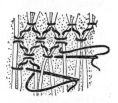

Pleats

The three main types of pleat are, knife pleats, inverted pleats and box pleats. For each pleat allow three times as much material as its depth, that is, 9″ of material will be needed for a pleat 3″ deep.

KNIFE PLEATS

These are sharp pleats which all lie in the same direction. The material is marked out, as in the diagram, with tack lines which *MUST* be on

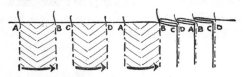

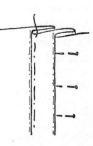

the straight grain. If necessary, draw a thread as a guide for the first tack line.

A to B and C to D are twice the depth of the

pleat while B to C is once the depth. Line A is folded over to line B and C over to D to form the pleats. Pin the pleats across into position and tack securely with silk. Press very lightly while the tacking is still in and remove it before the final pressing, otherwise an impression may be left.

FLARED KNIFE PLEATS

These pleats cannot be tacked on the straight grain as the fold of the pleat is off the grain on account of the flare. The fold does not stay in position quite so well, it is inclined to stretch and for this reason the edge of the fold is often stitched to keep it sharp.

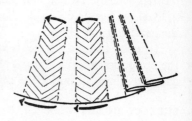

INVERTED PLEATS

An inverted pleat is a pair of knife pleats which are turned to face each other. These pleats are tacked out as for knife pleats but the spaces are all equal to the full depth of the pleat. Line A is folded to B and line C is also folded to B to meet A. Pin and tack.

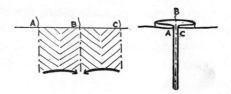

BOX PLEATS

A box pleat is the reverse side of an inverted pleat. The spaces between the tacking lines are equal to the full depth of the pleat. Pleat B over to A and C over to D. BC is the top of the pleat.

STITCHING PLEATS

The presser foot of the machine is inclined to push the top layer of material along slightly on the under one, so that, in order to prevent a pucker forming at the base of the stitching, all pleats and tucks should be stitched from the bottom upwards.

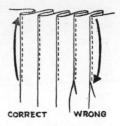

CORRECT   WRONG

JOINS IN PLEATS

If the pattern piece is too wide to be cut out of the width of the material, it will be necessary to arrange a join in the pleat. Plan the join to come inside the pleat, preferably on the inner fold as at A. Or it may be planned to come on the inner folds of the pleat as at B.

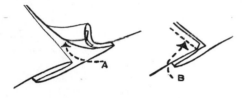

For economical cutting, an inverted pleat may have a separate underlay. This necessitates joins at each inner fold of the pleat.

Whenever there is a join in a pleat the hem needs special treatment to avoid bulk and to keep the edge of the pleat sharp.

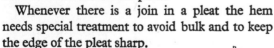

Treatment of hem

1) Unpick the seam at the hem as far as the hemline. See A.

2) Turn the hem up.

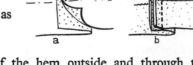

3) Stitch the unpicked ends of the hem outside and through the seam as at B. Thin down the two inner turnings and oversew the outer ones together.

Tucks

Tucks are really small pleats which are stitched for their entire length. The allowance of material is the same as for pleats.

PIN TUCKS

These are tiny tucks, the width of a pin, about $\frac{1}{16}$".

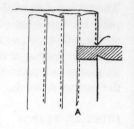

1) Fold the material on the straight grain for the first tuck, and stitch on the edge, on the top side.

2) Turn the tuck towards the left as at A. Use a marker, for the distance apart, and fold the material under at the notch. Stitch the next tuck on the folded edge.

WIDE TUCKS have to be tacked. Make two notches in a marker, one for the depth of the tuck and the second for the space between.

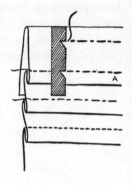

1) Fold the material on the straight grain R.S. out. (If necessary draw a thread as a guide.) Tack the first tuck.

2) Turn the tuck back as at A and place the lower notch on the marker to the tack line. Fold the material under level at the end of the marker and tack the next tuck level with the upper notch. When all the tucks are tacked, machine or run them by hand.

CROSS TUCKING

Tuck the material before cutting out. Stitch the tucks all one way first and then turn the work and stitch them the other way.

SHELL TUCKS

Tack the tucks as for wide tucks, making them $\frac{3}{16}$" deep.

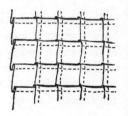

1) Make three small running stitches through the tack line.

2) Put the needle over the edge and behind and through the tuck and make a loop stitch with the cotton under the point. Pull the thread tight and make a backstitch to hold it.

Darts

In this case fullness is disposed of in a practical, rather than a decorative way.

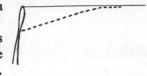

Stitch all darts from the wide end towards the point making the last four stitches lie absolutely on the fold. Fasten off securely.

When material is thick cut the fold of the dart almost to the end and press it open flat.

When a dart is tapered at both ends, snip it across in the centre to make it set flat. Neaten the cut ends with blanket stitch.

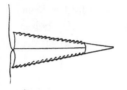

VIII : Edges

Raw edges may be finished in many ways, invisibly and decoratively. Curved edges, such as necks and armholes, are frequently neatened with crossway facings and bindings, as material cut on the cross becomes elastic, stretching and contracting to fit curves smoothly.

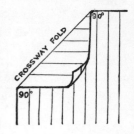

TO CUT ON THE CROSS fold the material so that the selvedge threads lie *EXACTLY* parallel to the weft threads. The fold is then on the true cross. Cut along the fold, being careful not to stretch the material nor to jag the edge.

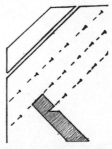

TO CUT THE STRIPS needed for facings and bindings, use a cardboard marker with a notch cut to the required depth, and mark out the strips with pins or tacking. *NEVER* use chalk for it drags the material so that when it springs back the strips are not an even width all the way along. Accurate measuring is *ESSENTIAL* for good results and saves time in the end. Cut the strips carefully along the pin lines.

To obtain the required length it is often necessary to join strips. As the joins are stitched on the straight grain of the material, make certain that the ends of each strip are cut along a straight thread. Remember that all joins must slant in the same direction and if they are made along the thinner weft threads of the material they are less noticeable.

TO JOIN CROSSWAY STRIPS

1) With the R.S. uppermost, place the ends parallel to each other.

2) Pick up the left-hand strip and turn it over onto the right-hand one so that the R.S. are inside and the strips form the corner of a square.

Slide the top strip up for ⅛″ and stitch the join across ¼″ below the raw edges, from where the points overlap.

3) Press the seam open and cut off the projecting points. When joining several strips, machine them one after the other and cut the stitching between afterwards.

Note. When crossway strips have to be joined in a circle, as for false hems, allow a ½″ turning at the beginning and stitch the strip round the garment until the two ends meet. Fold each turning back on a straight thread so that they just meet. Crease both folds sharply and stitch the ends together through the crease lines as for crossway strips.

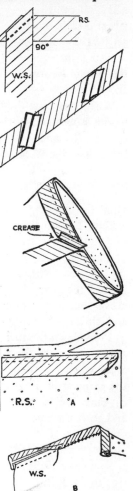

Crossway Binding

This is a decorative way of finishing an edge. The finished depth of the binding may be from ⅛″ to ¼″.

1) Cut the crossway strip four times the finished depth. Place the R.S. of the strip to the R.S. of the garment with the top edge level with the fitting line. *DO NOT PIN.* Stretch the strip round concave curves and ease it over convex curves. Tack and stitch a quarter of the depth of the strip below the fitting line. Cut away the turning of the garment.

2) Turn to the W.S. and press the strip upwards. Turn the top edge of the strip over to meet the other edges. Fold over once more and hem the fold to the previous stitches.

Binding Corners

When stitching the crossway strip on, take it straight across inside corners, as at A in the diagram. This makes the outer edge of the strip curl up. At outer corners, make a small pleat in the strip to enable

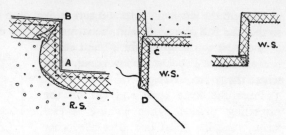

it to fit round the corner comfortably. Let the pleat stand up and take the stitching through the base only, see B.

When hemming the binding to the W.S. make corresponding pleats in the strip at outer corners, see C; but hem it straight across inner corners. To make an inner corner sharp, stitch a small dart in the binding on the W.S. and press it hard over to one side as at D.

Crossway Facing

Used for applying collars and cuffs and for finishing raw edges, invisibly. The usual finished depth is $\frac{3}{8}''$.

1) Cut crossway strips twice the finished depth.
2) Place the R.S. of the strip to the R.S. of the garment with a quarter of its depth beyond the fitting line. Ease round concave curves and stretch round convex ones. Tack and stitch on the fitting line.
3) Press down the turning of the strip only, as this will make the seam come just to the W.S. when the strip is turned over. Trim the garment turnings to $\frac{1}{8}''$.
4) Turn the strip completely to the W.S. and turn the raw edge under to meet the other edges. Tack in position and hem invisibly to the garment. Press well.

Sometimes facings are applied the reverse way to the R.S. of garments as a decorative finish.

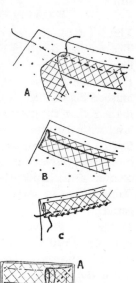

Facing Corners

Tack the strip to the garment making pleats in it at the inner corners and taking it straight round outer corners. Press over the turning on the free edge of the strip and then stitch darts at all the corners to make it lie flat as at A and B. Trim the darts and press the seams open. Turn the facing to the W.S. and tack and hem in position.

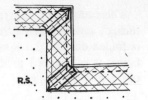

Piping

This is a decorative finish for edges and seams.

1) Cut crossway strips, twice the required depth of the piping plus turnings.
2) Fold the strip in half lengthwise R.S. outside. Using a marker, tack the edges together the desired depth from the fold.
3) Pin the piping to the R.S. of the garment with the tack line along the fitting line and the folded edge inside it.
4) Tack together through the fitting line.
5) Sandwich the piping between the two layers of the garment, matching all fitting lines. Pin, tack and stitch through the fitting lines.

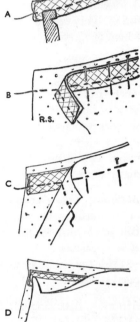

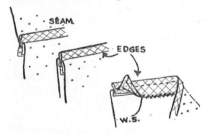

To neaten the back when the piping is in a seam, refer to the chapter on seams.

When the piping finishes a raw edge, trim the two inner turnings to $\frac{1}{8}''$ and the outer one to $\frac{1}{2}''$. Turn under the raw edge of the $\frac{1}{2}''$ turnings and hem invisibly to the garment, see diagram.

Frilled Edges

Frills are a decorative method of finishing edges and may be applied in many ways.

There are four main types of frill, pleated, tucked, gathered and flared. Unless the frill is folded double, the lower edge is finished before it is attached to the garment in one of the following ways.

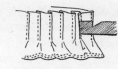

Method 1. The frill is attached with crossway binding. This is suitable for neck and cuff edges.

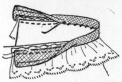

Method 2. The frill is applied with a crossway facing. This can be used when the frill ends a hem or sleeve.

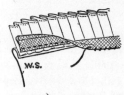

Method 3. Is used for collars and cuffs and when a frill is inserted in a seam. It resembles piping as the frill is enclosed between two layers of material.

w.s.

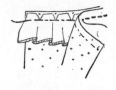

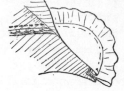

Method 4. Fold the garment turnings under on the fitting line and lay the fold on the frill level with the lower gathering thread, R.S. uppermost. Tack and stitch together.

Trim the turnings to ¼″ and neaten with blanket stitch.

Method 5. Attaching a frill with entredeux.
1) Place the frill, R.S. up to the W.S. of the garment. Place the entredeux over the frill with the R.S. inside. Tack and stitch through all thicknesses.

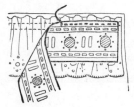

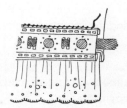

2) Turn the frill down and the entredeux up onto the R.S. of the garment. Turn in the raw edge, tack and slip-stitch or machine to position.

Finishing Edges with Lace

INSERTING ENTREDEUX

1) Trim away the edges and place the R.S. of the entredeux to the R.S. of the garment.

2) Roll the raw edge of the garment between the finger and thumb and whip it to the entredeux through the squares of the beading.

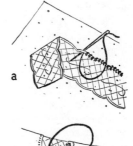

a

INSERTING LACE

1) Tack the lace insertion into position on the R.S. of the material.

2) With silk or fine matching cotton, oversew the edges of the lace very closely to the material.

3) Remove the tacking and trim away the material behind the lace, leaving ⅛" turnings. Roll the raw edges of these turnings and whip over them closely.

b

METHODS OF ATTACHING LACE AND NET TO RAW EDGES

1. *Lace whipped to edge*

Trim the turnings of the garment to ⅛". Tack the R.S. of the lace to the R.S. of the garment with the edge along the fitting line.

On the W.S. roll the garment edge and whip it to the lace. Lace may also be whipped to a finished edge.

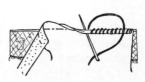

2. *Lace attached by machine*

Make a very small hem on the W.S. of the garment. On the R.S. place the edge of the lace on top of the hem and tack it. Run the lace on by hand or machine it on.

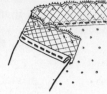

3. *Lace applied with blanket stitch*

Roll and whip the raw edge of the garment.

On the R.S. of the garment lap the lace $\frac{1}{4}''$ over the rolled edge. Tack it in position. Work fine blanket stitch over the edge of the lace and through the garment.

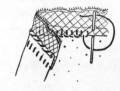

4. *Lace applied with satin stitch*

Tack the lace in position on the R.S. of the garment.

Hold a thread of twist over the lower edge of the lace and work satin stitch closely over it and through the lace and material.

On the W.S. cut the garment turnings away to the stitching.

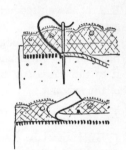

Edge finished with net, using pin stitch

1) Place the raw edges of the folded net over the edge of the garment on the R.S. and tack securely.

2) Work pin stitch, or any other suitable decorative stitch, through the net and the material on the fitting line.

A

3) Cut away the surplus material turnings at the back and the turnings of the net on the R.S.

B

Note. When joining lace by this method, the stitch is worked over the finished edge of the lace and there is nothing to cut away.

Appliqué and Découpé

These processes are both worked with contrasting materials. The contrast may be in colour or in texture, such as net and silk or satin and a dull surfaced material.

In appliqué the contrasting material is stitched on top of the other one and in découpé it is applied underneath and the top part is cut away to reveal it. Both methods are used in the following example which shows net joined to an edge with satin stitch.

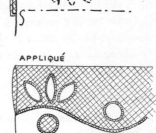

APPLIQUÉ

1) Tack double net behind the edge of the garment, leaving turnings deep enough to cover the entire pattern. Tack together.

2) Outline the pattern with small running stitches through all layers of material.

3) Work the pattern closely with satin stitch.

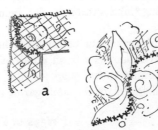

DÉCOUPÉ

4) On the top side, cut away the unwanted material close to the stitching. (Appliqué.) On the underside, cut away the unwanted net. (Découpé.)

Joining Lace

ALL-OVER LACE

1) With the R.S. uppermost, overlap the pieces to be joined matching the pattern. Pin and tack.

2) Oversew closely round the pattern's outline and then oversew back crossing the previous stitches.

3) Cut away the surplus material to the stitching on both sides.

a   b

JOINING LACE FOR A 'V' NECK

a   b

1) To form the V fold a dart in the lace as in the diagram. Oversew the inner fold of the dart.

2) Cut away the dart to within $\frac{1}{8}''$ of the stitching. Oversew back crossing the previous stitches.

F

Hems

LEVELLING THE HEM

1) The wearer should stand firmly and evenly on both feet.

2) Use a proper hem marker or a yard stick and mark the hem line with chalk or pins the required distance off the ground. If pins are used, they should be placed about 4″ apart.

3) Mark the hem line more permanently with a line of flat tacking.

TURNING UP THE HEM

4) Lay the garment flat on the table R.S. out. Turn the hem up on the tack line and pin vertically at intervals.

5) Tack through $\frac{1}{4}$″ up from the folded edge.

6) With a cardboard marker, mark off the depth of the hem with a line of tacking taken through the hem turning only.

The maximum depth for a hem is 4″. This amount is left on children's dresses for letting down purposes and 2″ is the usual allowance for adult garments.

Ways of Finishing Hems

PLAIN HEM, METHOD I

This is suitable for thin material only.

1) Trim away the surplus hem, leaving $\frac{1}{4}$″ turnings beyond the tack line.

2) If the skirt is flared the edge of the hem will be wider than the part onto which it is turned up. Pleats will have to be made at intervals to dispose of the fullness. Avoid making these pleats very near a seam. If the material is woollen, this fullness is shrunk away under a damp cloth, in which case the depth of the hem is not marked off until after the shrinking.

3) Turn the raw edge under to the tack line. Tack and slip stitch to position.

PLAIN HEM, METHOD 2

1) Edge-stitch the hem on the depth line of tacking. Trim the turnings to $\frac{1}{4}''$.
2) Tack the stitched edge in position and slip hem it.

HEM FOR A CIRCULAR SKIRT

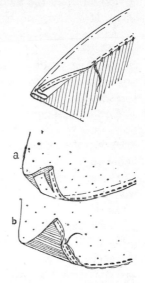

This hem is only $\frac{1}{8}''$ deep otherwise there would be too much fullness to disperse owing to the large flare.

1) Mark the level of the hem with tacking.
2) Place the garment under the machine R.S. uppermost. With the help of a pair of scissors turn the hem under $\frac{1}{8}''$ below the tack line. Machine on the extreme edge.
3) Trim the turning down to the stitching, as at *a* in diagram.
4) With the R.S. uppermost, turn the machined edge under to the hemline with the point of the scissors and again machine on the edge, as at *b*.

Hems for Heavier Materials

HERRINGBONED HEM

Flannel garments and corduroy may have this type of hem.

1) Cut the hem to the actual required depth.
2) Tack the hem in position and fix it by working herringbone stitch over the raw edge.

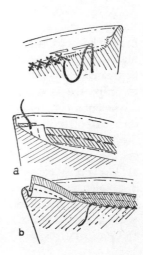

HEM FIXED WITH PARIS BINDING

This method is used for heavy woollens and bouncy materials.

1) Shrink away any fullness and mark the hem depth with a line of tacking.
2) Place the top edge of the Paris binding to this tack line. Pin and tack it to the hem only.

Machine the lower edge of the binding to the hem.

3) Trim the hem down to half the depth of the binding.

4) Pin and tack the binding in position and invisibly hem to the garment. *Note.* Crossway binding may be used for this hem.

FALSE HEM

When skirt lengths alter and children grow, false hems can be used to lengthen dresses.

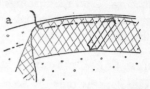

1) Let the hem down to its full extent and press out the crease. Mark the new hem level with a tack line, leaving ¾" turnings below it.

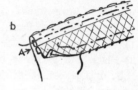

2) Cut crossway strips, from 1" to 3" wide, from matching material and join them to obtain the required length.

3) Place the strip to the hem, R.S. together, and tack and machine ½" outside the hemline.

4) Press the seam open.

5) Turn up the hem on the hemline and tack ¼" above the fold.

6) Turn the raw edge in ¼" and tack and slip hem to the garment.

Turning Out Edges

Some garments have shaped edges which have to be faced. Before the facings can be turned to the inside, the turnings have to be treated according to the shape.

1) Snip the turnings completely off across outer corners so that the point will turn out sharply, see A in the diagram. Snip quite into inner corners or they will not turn out at all, see B.

2) The outer edge of concave curves is tighter than the part on to which it has to be turned. Snip across the turnings to the stitching at intervals as at C, and the cuts will spread out.

3) Convex curves have larger outer edges and the turnings should have

small wedge shaped pieces cut out of them, otherwise they will pleat and
be bulky when turned out, see D. Trim turnings to $\frac{1}{8}''$.

The following diagrams show the method of treating the edges of a
revers facing on a blouse.

The concave, convex edges and the points are dealt with, see A,
B, C and D. When the facing is turned inside, the seam below the top
buttonhole should be just inside and, above this buttonhole, it should be
just under the rever. To do this, press the turning of the facing only,
back as at E to the buttonhole, and round the revers, press back the
turning of the garment, before turning the facing to the inside.
Note how the turnings are cut at the hem edge of the facing.

Revers Facing

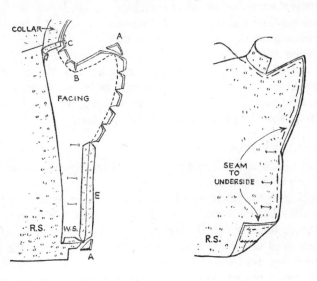

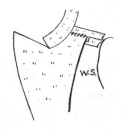

Finishing Edges with Fringes

Fringes are used on table runners, stoles and pockets as a fashion feature and on other household articles.

1. *Fringe worked on a raw edge*

Measure the required depth of the fringe up from the raw edge and at that level draw out 4 or 5 threads from the material. Work hem stitch along the upper edge of the drawn threads and then withdraw all the threads below making the fringe, see diagram.

2. *Fringe worked on a hemmed edge*

Cut several lengths of wool or silk a little longer than the required depth of the fringe. Put them together and fold in half. Insert a fine crochet hook through the hem of the article from the underside and hook the looped end of the fringe through the material. Slip the cut ends of the wool through the loop and pull tight as in the diagram. For a more interesting effect half the thread from one group may be knotted to half from the next group. Trim the cut ends level.

CORDS AND TASSELS

Cords are useful as dressing-gown belts and for edging cushion covers and other household articles.

According to the thickness of cord required, cut several lengths of wool or silk three times the desired finished length. Tie them together at each end. Insert a pencil in each end and twist them in opposite directions until the whole length is tightly twisted. Loop the centre over something fixed such as a nail or hook in a wall and holding the cord taut bring the two pencils together. Unhook the centre and the cord will twist up automatic-ally. Short cords can be man-aged by one person but a long one will need two people to make it.

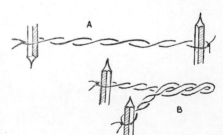

Cords are often finished off with tassels and these are easily made. Cut a piece of card a little longer than the required length of the tassel and wind silk or wool round it many times as in the diagram. Slip a short thread through at the top and tie it tightly in a reef knot. At the base cut the threads through and remove the card. A little below the top wind another thread tightly round the tassel and fasten it off by taking it through with a needle several times.

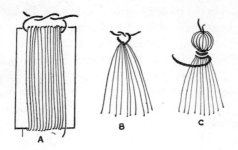

IX: Pressing

Press as you sew is the golden rule in needlework. In fact it is necessary to press before starting to sew. To avoid disappointment when garments are laundered or cleaned, woollen materials and some cottons should be shrunk before cutting out. Cottons may be immersed in cold water for a few hours, dried and ironed while slightly damp. Woollen material may be left overnight wrapped in a damp sheet and then pressed dry on the wrong side under a cloth. The more usual and quicker method is to damp press it.

DAMP PRESSING

Place the material on the ironing board folded in half, as it is bought.
1) Dip a pressing cloth into a bowl of water and wring it out well.
2) Lay the damp cloth over the material and press a hot iron up and down all over it. DO NOT IRON, only press. Lift the cloth and pat the steam away with the hand.
3) Dry the material off by passing the iron very lightly over the surface using no pressure at all.
4) Damp press the material all over to shrink it evenly and then turn it over and shrink the underside. The pressing cloth needs repeated damping as it is necessary to create steam.

RULES FOR PRESSING

1) Always see that the iron is clean and test the temperature on a spare piece of material before using it on the garment, as different materials require different temperatures.
2) Press on the wrong side of material.
3) Press woollen materials under a damp cloth. Other materials seldom need this and, on some rayons, a permanent water mark could result from the use of it. Press under a dry cloth when the iron may cause shininess or leave an impression.
4) Press all seams after stitching. It is especially important to press one seam before joining it to another, to obtain a flat finish.
5) Press very lightly over tackings for they may leave imprints which are difficult to remove.

PRESSING DIFFERENT MATERIALS

Cottons and linens require a hot iron for good results. If it should be necessary to use a damp cloth, make sure the material is completely dried off as cottons and linens are liable to mildew if left damp. Seersuckers should be pressed as little as possible and very lightly as the crinkled effect may press out, but it will come back with damping. The appearance of drip dry and 'minimum iron' cottons is improved with pressing but in these, and in crease resisting materials, it is not always possible to press seams really flat and sometimes it is not easy to obtain sharp edges on pleats.

Woollen materials. Use a warm iron and a damp cloth and press on the wrong side. The iron is apt to leave a shiny imprint unless a cloth is used. If the material does become shiny, the steam caused by pressing under a really damp cloth should remove it. If the iron is hot it may damage the material and cause it to mat up.

Silks require a moderately hot iron and quick pressing. Do not damp shantung and tussore as they become papery and acquire permanent water marks.

Rayons. Some rayons can be quite tricky to press and a spare piece must be tested first. Never use a damp cloth for it may cause water marks. Use a cool iron as a hot one can cause permanent damage. Always press on the wrong side and never heavily. Should it be necessary to press on the right side at any time, do not press over seams as imprints may be left which cannot be removed.

Nylon and terylene fabrics. Owing to the crease resisting properties of these materials, it is not always easy to press seams quite flat. Use a COOL iron and avoid pressing in unwanted creases as these can only be removed with a hotter iron and a really hot iron can melt the material away.

Mixtures of fibres. When a material is made of two or more fibres, for example, wool and cotton, treat for the more delicate one, in this case wool.

Cotton velveteen, silk and nylon velvets. All these materials should be pressed on the wrong side over a velvet board in order not to flatten the pile. If this is not available, stand the iron up on end and pass the part to be pressed back and forth over its surface. Fingermarks on velvet can be removed by holding the material in the steam of a fast boiling kettle.

Corduroy needs no special care other than pressing on the wrong side.

Embroidery. Place embroidery right side down on a soft pad and press the wrong side under a damp or dry cloth, according to the nature of the material. This raises the embroidery on the right side.

PRESSING DIFFERENT PARTS OF A GARMENT

Gathers. Run the tip of the iron up into the gathering threads.

Plain seams. Press the seam double first, then open it and press over a wooden roller which will leave no impression on the right side. A cookery rolling pin will answer the purpose.

French seams. Press fairly heavily on the wrong side, then lift the seam and run the tip of the iron underneath to press out any imprint.

Darts. Press as for French or plain seams, according to whether they are double or cut open.

Press shoulder darts towards the neck.

Press underarm darts downwards.

Press elbow darts downwards.

Press waist darts towards the centre front and centre back.

Plain sleeveheads. Place a round pad, special glove pad or folded towel under the sleevehead and run the tip of the iron towards the shoulder pressing away any puckering at this part. If the material is woollen the fullness can be shrunk away under a damp cloth. Press the armhole seam over towards the sleeve, moving the sleevehead round on the pad.

Waist seams. If convenient these may be pressed open, otherwise press them up on to the bodice.

Hems. When the tacking is removed, press the lower edge heavily and the top of the hem more lightly so that it does not show on the right side of the garment.

Tucks. Press on the wrong side. Run the back of pin tucks over an upturned iron to raise them.

Pleats. Remove the tacking and press under a damp cloth heavily. Dry off by pressing again under a piece of dry muslin.

Fasteners. Do not press over hooks and eyes, press studs and zips as an impression will be left.

SEQUENCE OF THE FINAL PRESSING

1) Press collars and revers.
2) Press sleeves.
3) Press the bodice and waist seam.
4) Press the skirt.
5) Press any loose or attached belts.

This order is followed to avoid creasing any parts already pressed.

X : Collars

Collars are either straight or curved and are made up as follows.

Straight Type Collars

1) Place the two collar pieces together with the W.S. outside. Pin, tack and stitch through the fitting lines. Note that the stitching in this type of collar begins and ends at the tailor tacks marked B on the diagram.

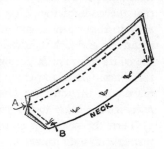

2) Trim the turnings to $\frac{1}{8}''$ and cut them across the corners so that the points may turn out sharply. See A.

3) Press the turnings down on the underside of the collar only. This will make the seam fall slightly to the underside when the collar is turned right side out, making it invisible in wear.

4) Turn the collar out and tack round the edge to keep the seam slightly underneath.

Curved Peter Pan Collars

1) Stitch through the fitting lines on the W.S.
2) Cut wedge shaped pieces out of the turnings at intervals round the curved edge. This prevents the turnings pleating when the collar is turned out.

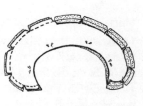

3) Press down the turnings of the underside.
4) Turn the collar out and tack round the edge.

Applying a Straight Collar

Before the collar is applied the front facing of the garment must be dealt with.

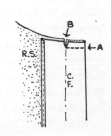

1) Fold the front facing to the R.S. of the garment and stitch through the fitting lines

as in the diagram from A as far as B
which is the centre front. Trim the
turning to $\frac{1}{8}''$ and snip right across it to
B. Turn the facing out to the W.S.

2) Place the top side of the collar to the
W.S. of the garment. Match the fitting
lines and pin vertically. Make certain
that the ends of the collar come exactly to the centre fronts of the garment. Pin and tack the topside only of
the collar to the neck through the fitting lines. Check the collar points to
make sure they are the same length.
Machine the collar to the neck.

3) Turn the collar up and press the
turnings up onto it inside.

4) On the R.S. fold under the turning
on the free edge of the collar. Pin, tack
and hem this edge to the machine
stitching. The collar turns over and hides this hemming.

Mandarin Collar

This type of collar is placed to the R.S. of the garment in (2) above
and the hemming is worked on the inside of the neck edge so that it
will not show.

Shirt Collar with a Band

1) Make up the collar.

2) At the neck edge of *one* of the collar band pieces fold the turning to
the W.S. on the fitting line and tack it.

3) Sandwich the collar between the
two pieces of the band, right sides inside, so that the ends of the collar lie on
the centre front tacks. Match all the
fitting lines and pin, tack and machine
through them, from one end of the
band to the other.

4) Press the band downwards, away
from the collar.

5) Place the unfolded turning of the

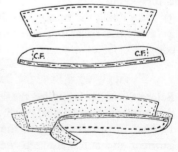

band to the neck edge on the W.S. of the garment.

Note that the ends of the band come quite to the ends of the wrap.

Pin, tack and stitch the fitting lines together.

6) Press the turnings up inside the band.

7) Tack the free folded edge to cover the previous stitching and machine it in place.

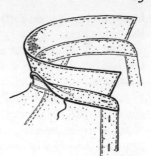

Revers Collar

1) Place the collar in position on the R.S. of the garment with the ends to the centre fronts. Pin the underside of the collar to the neck edge.

2) Tack and stitch through the fitting lines, across the back neck from one shoulder to the other only.

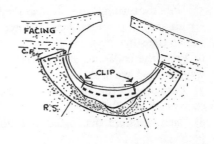

3) Fold the front facings of the garment over to the R.S. on the wrap line enclosing the free ends of the collar. Make sure the ends of the collar are the same depth. Pin and tack through all four thicknesses.

4) Machine through the fitting lines from the wrap edge to each shoulder seam to meet the ends of the stitching across the back neck.

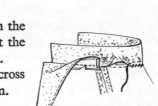

5) Trim the turnings to ⅛″ and snip across them to the stitching at each shoulder seam.

6) Turn the facings to the inside.

7) Fold the turnings under on the free part of the collar. Tack and hem this edge to the previous stitching enclosing all turnings.

Applying a Peter Pan Collar

1) Place the collar in position on the right side of the garment matching the centre backs and making the ends of the collar touch the centre

front tack line. Pin on vertically and tack through the fitting lines.

2) Fold the front facings of the garment over to the R.S. on the wrap line enclosing the collar ends.

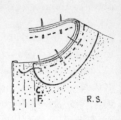

3) Cut a crossway strip of material $\frac{3}{4}''$ to $1''$ wide and lay it, R.S. down, over the fitting line on the collar, as in the diagram, with the ends extending just over the edges of the wrap.

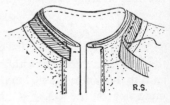

4) Tack and machine through the fitting lines.

5) Trim the turnings to $\frac{1}{8}''$ and, as they are curved, snip across them at intervals to the stitching.

6) Press the collar up and the crossway facing down with the iron.

7) Turn under the raw edge of the strip making it $\frac{3}{8}''$ deep.

8) Tack and hem the folded edge in position.

Roll Collar

This collar is cut in one piece with the front bodice.

1) Place the two fronts together R.S. inside. Pin, tack and machine across the short seam at the centre back neck. Trim the turnings to $\frac{1}{4}''$ and press them open.

2) Clip the turnings to the fitting line at A in the diagram. Prepare the facings in the same way.

3) Join the back and front shoulder seams and press them open.

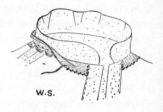

4) Join the back neck of the collar part to the back neck of the garment. Press the turnings up on to the collar.

5) Open out flat and place the R.S. of the facings to the R.S. of the garment. Pin, tack and machine through the fitting lines.

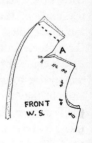

6) Trim the turnings to $\frac{1}{8}''$ and press them open.

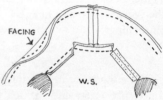

7) Turn the facings to the inside of the garment. Tack round the outside edge and press lightly.

8) Turn under the raw edge of the facing at the neck and tack and hem to the previous stitching.

9) Hem the ends of the facing to the shoulder seams.

Setting a Collar into a Lined Yoke

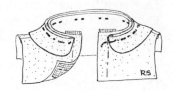

1) Trim the turnings of the collar and yoke to $\frac{1}{4}''$.

2) Place the collar in position on the R.S. of the yoke. Tack through the fitting lines.

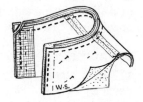

3) Tack a strip of organdie behind the button and buttonhole positions down the centre fronts of the yoke.

4) Place the R.S. of the lining over the yoke, enclosing the collar between them. Smooth down and pin across at intervals.

5) Tack and stitch up the fronts and round the neck through all thicknesses, on the fitting line.

6) Snip across the neck turnings to the stitching at intervals and trim off the corners.

7) Turn the lining to the inside. Turn the collar up and push the yoke down.

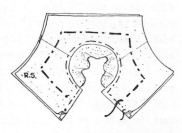

Tack the lining to the yoke up the front edges and immediately below the collar. Lay flat on the table and tack together again through the centre.

XI : Openings

Openings enable the wearer to get into a garment easily. They may be made at the neck, in the left underarm side seam or at the wrist. They must be made very strongly to avoid any possibility of splitting. The length of an opening depends on its position and on the tightness of the garment. The table at the end of this chapter will act as a guide.

Continuous Opening

This is one of the strongest openings and is used frequently on children's clothes. It is a binding of straight material and may be worked in a slit or in a seam. The finished width of the binding for a skirt opening is $1''$, for a dress $\frac{3}{4}''$ and for wrist and neck openings $\frac{1}{2}''$.

METHOD FOR A CONTINUOUS OPENING IN A SLIT

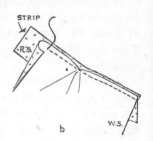

1) Cut a straight strip of material (selvedge way if possible) twice as long as the opening by twice the finished width of the binding plus $\frac{1}{4}''$ for turnings.

2) Holding the W.S. of the garment towards one, place the R.S. of the strip to the R.S. of the opening with the edges together. Tack $\frac{1}{8}''$ from the edge to within $\frac{1}{2}''$ of the base of the opening, then slide the garment down on the strip until the base of the opening is $\frac{1}{8}''$ below the strip edge. Continue tacking $\frac{1}{8}''$ below the strip edge and catch in the last uncut thread at the base of the opening. Then taper the garment back for $\frac{1}{2}''$ until the edges meet again. Continue tacking to the end. This is very important as no turning is allowed at the base of the opening and $\frac{1}{8}''$ turnings must be kept all along the strip to make the finished width uniform.

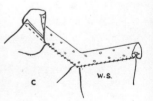

3) Machine or run by hand on the tack line.

4) Press the turnings up on to the strip and

then fold the strip through the centre to the W.S.

5) Fold the raw edge under ⅛", and tack and hem it to the previous stitching. Press well.

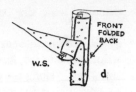

METHOD FOR OPENING IN A SEAM

1) At the base of the opening cut across the garment turnings as far as the seam stitching.

2) Cut a strip twice as long as the opening by twice the finished width plus 1" for turnings.

3) With the right sides together tack the strip to the garment on the fitting line. Take extreme care to avoid a gap at the base of the opening.

4) Trim the turnings to ⅛" (¼" if the material frays badly) and finish as for the opening in a slit, turning the raw edge under ½".

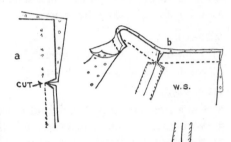

Note. When this opening is used in the side seam of a dress or petticoat the free ends have to be joined. Arrange for this join to come on the underlap where there is not a seam in the garment. This avoids bulk. See diagram.

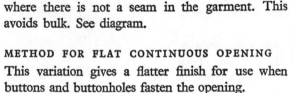

METHOD FOR FLAT CONTINUOUS OPENING

This variation gives a flatter finish for use when buttons and buttonholes fasten the opening.

The finished width of the binding is 1".

1) Cut the strip and sew it on as for the continuous opening.

2) Fold the strip through the centre to the W.S. Turn the raw edge under and press well.

3) On the underwrap side only, tack and hem the free edge to the previous

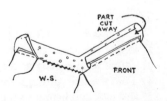

G

stitching from the base of the opening to the top.

4) On the top side cut away the under part of the strip, as illustrated, leaving $\frac{1}{4}''$ turnings at the base and $\frac{1}{8}''$ to $\frac{1}{4}''$ along the side.

5) Fold the strip completely over to the inside and tack it flat to the garment forming a facing.

6) Machine the facing to the garment down the free edge, across the base and up the outer edge.

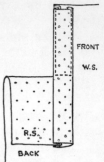

Dress Placket

This consists of a facing $\frac{3}{4}''$ wide on the top side and a binding $\frac{3}{4}''$ wide on the underside. The placket is usually 8″ long, 4″ above and 4″ below the waist line.

METHOD

1) Trim the turnings of the opening to $\frac{1}{4}''$. On the underside only, cut across the turnings to the stitching, $\frac{1}{2}''$ beyond each end of the opening.

Front facing

2) Cut a crossway strip 1″ wide and 1″ longer than the opening.

3) With the right sides together and the edges level, tack the strip to the front turning on the fitting line, arranging the extra length to extend $\frac{1}{2}''$ beyond each end of the opening.

4) Machine $\frac{1}{8}''$ outside the fitting line on the turning, for the whole length of the strip.

5) Press the strip over completely to the wrong side of the garment. Turn the raw edge in $\frac{1}{8}''$ and tack it flat to the garment. Invisibly hem in position. Press and remove the tacking.

The underwrap

6) Cut a crossway strip $1\frac{3}{4}''$ wide and 1″ longer than the opening.

7) Stitch it on exactly as for the front facing.

8) Fold the strip through the centre to the inside. Turn the raw edge in $\frac{1}{8}''$ and tack and hem it to the previous stitching, thus forming a binding $\frac{3}{4}''$ wide.

To neaten and strengthen the ends

Oversew the ends of the underwrap to those of the front facing. Fold the underwrap and the facing away from each other level with the end of the opening and oversew together very strongly inside the placket.

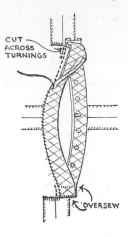

Sew a hook and bar at the waist seam to take the strain and fasten the rest of the opening with press studs 1″ to 1¼″ apart.

Skirt Placket

This opening is used on heavier materials. The usual length is 8″.

METHOD

Leave 1″ turnings on the garment. Cut a yard of Paris binding into four 9″ lengths, that is, 1″ longer than the opening.

Front side

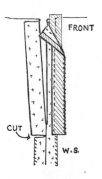

1) Place one piece of Paris binding to the W.S. of the skirt opening with the outer edge touching the fitting line and the extra 1″ extending below the opening. Tack it on with long loose stitches which must not show on the R.S. This is to strengthen the position of the press studs. Fold the front turning back over the binding.

2) Face the raw edge of the turning with another piece of Paris binding, which is machined to the turning on the outer edge and hemmed flat to the garment on the inner edge. Make the total width of the facing 1″ wide.

The underside

3) Tack a piece of Paris binding on the underside of the turning ⅛″ outside the fitting line.

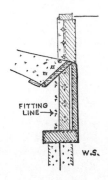

4) With the fourth piece of Paris binding, bind the raw edge as for crossway binding, taking it 1″ below the end of the opening. Cut the turnings across at the bottom of the binding as far as the seam stitching to release the underwrap so that it will fold over onto the front facing.

To neaten the base
Hem a small piece of Paris binding over the raw edges,
see diagram.

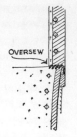

To strengthen the end
Fold the facing and the wrap away from each other,
level with the base of the opening, and oversew the two
together very strongly inside the opening.

Shirt Cuff and Box Pleat Opening

This opening is generally used at the wrist and as a short front opening
in shirts and blouses of the shirt type.

There are many ways of making it and the following method is a
simple one consisting of two straight bindings. The finished width
of the bindings for a wrist opening may be $\frac{3}{4}"$ to $1\frac{1}{4}"$ and the length,
from 3" to 6". For a neck opening the finished width may be $1\frac{1}{4}"$ to 2"
and the length, including the neck, must be not less than 22" for the
head to pass through easily.

Care must be taken to arrange the upper and underwraps on the
correct sides of the opening, remembering that girls' garments button
right over left and boys' the reverse way.

Sleeves fasten from the back over towards the underarm seam.

METHOD

1) Outline the shape on the garment by tacking round a paper pattern.
Leaving $\frac{1}{4}"$ turnings along the sides, cut away the
centre part inside the tack lines for the actual length
of the opening. Note that the material is not cut
away inside the pointed part as this extends beyond
the opening.

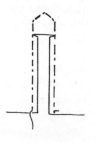

2) For the underwrap cut a straight piece of material
twice the finished width plus two $\frac{1}{4}"$ turnings, by
the length of the opening plus $\frac{1}{4}"$.

3) For the upper part cut a straight strip twice the
finished width plus two $\frac{1}{4}"$ turnings, by the length
of the opening plus the depth of the pointed part
plus $\frac{1}{4}"$. Using the paper pattern, tack the outline on one side of the
strip and cut away the part not wanted on the other side remembering
to leave $\frac{1}{4}"$ turnings everywhere.

4) Place the R.S. of the upper and underwrap in position on the W.S. of the garment,
with the extra length above the opening.
Tack and machine on the outline as far as
the top of the opening only.

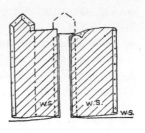

5) Fold the underwrap through the centre
to the R.S. Turn the raw edge in $\frac{1}{4}''$, then
tack and machine it down so that it just
covers the previous machine stitching.

6) Fold the upper part through the centre to
the R.S. Turn in the raw edges all round
$\frac{1}{4}''$ and tack to cover the previous stitching.
Begin machining at A just below the top of
the opening. Stitch across to B, then round
the point and down the inner side. The outer
edge is stitched separately to match. On the
W.S. there will be a raw edge below the
point. Neaten this with blanket stitch.

Note. As a neck opening this may be fastened with buttons and the
buttonholes always run vertically down the centre of the upper wrap.
A wrist opening is not fastened as the buttons are usually on the cuff.

Faced Opening

This is used for wrist and short neck openings when the opening is
in a slit. It is suitable for almost all types of material.

METHOD FOR A WRIST OPENING

1) Mark the position of the opening on the sleeve with a line of tacking,
but do not cut it.

2) For the facing cut a piece of material on the
same grain as the garment 2'' wide and $1\frac{1}{4}''$ longer
than the opening. Neaten the top and the two
side edges with edge stitching or oversewing to
match the rest of the garment.

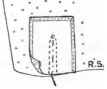

3) Place the R.S. of the facing to the R.S. of the
garment with the centre on the tackline and the
extra length at the top. Tack to the sleeve along
the tack mark.

4) Machine either side of the tack mark, $\frac{1}{8}''$ away at
the base tapering bluntly to nothing at the top.

5) Cut along the tack mark quite up to the
last stitch at the top.

6) Turn the facing through to the W.S.
Tack round the slit and press.

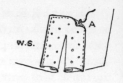

7) On the W.S. catch the top corners of the
facing invisibly to the garment.

Note. A neck facing is, as a rule, a shaped
piece which is supplied with a pattern. It is
put on in the same way. The base is inclined
to be a weak point which may split if strained.
This can be reinforced by placing a small
square of organdie over the base before machining the facing to the garment. See
diagram.

Full Length Box Pleat Opening for a Blouse

This opening has a hem on the underside, and on the top, an outside
facing, which may be 1″ to 1½″ wide, according to the style of the
blouse.

METHOD

1) Cut the facing the required width plus
two ½″ turnings, by the length of the blouse
front.

2) Tack a strip of organdie to the W.S. of
this facing. Put a tack line down the centre
of the facing. Along the inner edge, fold the
½″ turning to the W.S. over the organdie and
tack it down.

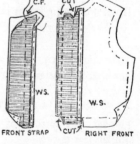

3) On the right hand front, place the R.S. of the facing to the W.S.
of the blouse, with the central tack line on the C.F. of the garment.
Tack and machine together on the fitting line, beginning at the C.F.
of the neck, then stitching down the outer edge and across the base
for the width of the facing.

4) Trim the turnings to ⅛″ and clip across them to the stitching on
the C.F. line at the neck, and level with the end of the facing at the
hem. This releases the turnings for the collar and allows the hem to
turn back on to the W.S.

5) Turn the facing completely over to the R.S. of the garment and
tack down the free edge. Machine down both edges.

6) On the left front of the blouse turn the raw edge under ¼″ and tack it. Fold this edge over to touch the centre front on the right side of the blouse. Stitch across at the neck edge, from the fold to the C.F. Trim the turnings to ⅛″ and clip across them on the C.F. line. Stitch across the hem edge and trim the turnings but do not clip them across.
7) Turn right side out. Tack and hem the free edge to position on the C.F. line, on the W.S.

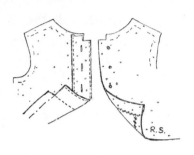

LEFT FRONT

Hemmed Sleeve Opening

This opening is inconspicuous and is made in the seam.
1) When cutting out allow 1¼″ turning at the opening on the front of the sleeve for the wrap.
2) At the top of the opening clip across the turning on the front of the sleeve as far as the seam stitching.
3) Fold the turning on the back of the sleeve to the W.S. on the fitting line. Turn the raw edge under and tack and hem it to the sleeve.
4) On the front of the sleeve fold the extra turning through the centre to make the wrap. Turn in the raw edge and tack and hem it to the fitting line.
5) Fold the wrap over on to the hem and machine through across the top of the opening.
6) Blanket stitch the clipped edges of the wrap and the turning to neaten them.

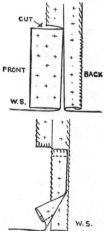

The Types of Openings and the Length
Suitable for Various Garments

Neck Openings

Dress, blouse or nightdress — Faced or box pleat types. Continuous for children's wear. The length including the neck to be not less than 22".

Side Openings Above and Below the Waist

Dress — Dress placket or zip fastener. Continuous for children. Length 8" (4" above and 4" below waist level). If the dress fits tightly or the material splits easily make it at least 12".

Full length petticoat — Continuous or flat continuous. Length 8" as for dress.

Small children's wear C.F. or C.B. — Faced or hemmed above the waist. Continuous or flat continuous below. Length nape to 4" or 6" below the waist.

Side Openings Below the Waist

Skirt — Dress placket for thin materials, continuous for children. Skirt placket for thicker types. Zip fastener. Length 8".

Shorts and slacks — Skirt placket or flat continuous. Zip fastener. Length 8".

Waist petticoat and knickers — Flat continuous. Length 6".

Girls' pyjama trousers — Flat continuous or continuous. Length 8" for one opening, 6" if there are two openings. For boys' pyjamas the opening is similar to the dress placket.

Wrist Openings

Dress, blouse or nightdress — Continuous or hemmed opening in the seam. Continuous, faced or shirt cuff type when in a slit. Length from 3" to 6".

XII: Fastenings

Of the many fastenings used in needlework, the button and buttonhole method is one of the most important. Before buttonholes are made, their size, position and the grain of the material have to be considered.

The size of buttonholes

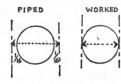

Worked buttonholes are made the exact diameter of the button, unless it is very thick or bumpy, when the size can only be determined by trying it out on a spare piece of material. Piped and bound buttonholes are made the diameter of the button plus $\frac{1}{8}''$ as they are not so strong and do not stretch so much in wear as the worked ones.

The grain of the material

Buttonholes should be cut along a straight thread of the material. Cut on the cross they will stretch. However, when a whole garment is cut on the cross, they cannot always be avoided and a strengthening strip of organdie, cut on the straight, must be inserted behind the position, and the buttonhole should be stranded by working two threads round it, taking a small stitch across each end, as in the diagram A. Work buttonhole stitch over the stranding.

Material which frays can make the working of buttonholes difficult. When this happens, machine round the tack line marking the position, $\frac{1}{16}''$ above and below it, before cutting the buttonhole, and then oversew the cut edges together. See B.

Buttonholes on single material are neither strong nor easy to work and are never used. When they have to be worked where the material is single, for example, when they are used as belt slots, a piece of matching material with the raw edges neatened, or a piece of tape, must be tacked behind the position and the buttonhole worked through both thicknesses.

Direction of buttonholes

As a rule buttonholes are placed so that the outer end takes the strain of the button. Usually they are horizontal unless they take the strain of shoulder straps or are the means of fastening children's skirts and trousers to their blouses and shirts, when they are placed vertically. They are also vertical when a garment has a strap facing on the R.S. down the centre front, as on a man's shirt, in order that the buttons may remain in the centre of the strap when fastened.

Horizontal buttonholes have the outer end rounded to take the shank of the button and the inner end square to hold the edges together and to prevent it splitting in wear. Vertical buttonholes have either two round or two square ends, whichever is preferred.

Position for buttonholes and buttons

Whether they fasten at the front or at the back, ladies' clothes button from the right hand side over to the left. Therefore the buttonholes are worked on the right hand side. Men's clothes fasten over the opposite way.

1) The outer end of the buttonhole lies on the centre front line of the garment because the button always slides to the end of the buttonhole and this will bring it to the centre of the garment.

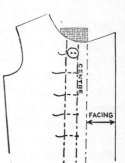

Note the centre front line must not be less than half the diameter of the button away from the edge of the garment, so that when, fastened, the button will not extend beyond the edge.

2) Tack a strengthening strip of organdie, cut on the straight, behind the position.

3) Mark the centre front of the garment with a line of tacking. Mark the width of the buttonhole with another tack line inside the centre front.

4) Mark, with tacking the position of the top and bottom buttonholes and then divide the space between evenly according to the number of buttons.

Marking out vertical buttonholes

1) Interline the box-pleat facing with organdie.

2) With pins, mark the position and the depth of the buttonhole on the centre front line.

3) Mark all the buttonholes in this way, spacing them evenly.
4) Cut the buttonhole between the pins on the centre front line.

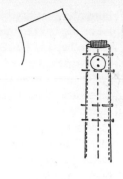

The position of the buttons
1) Tack a strip of organdie behind the position.
2) Tack in the centre front line.
3) When all the buttonholes have been worked, lap them over the button side matching the centre front lines.
4) Put pins through the outer ends of the buttonholes and through the centre front of the button side as in the diagram.

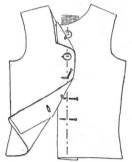

Buttonholes on cuffs
Cuffs button from the underside over towards the front. The space between the edge of the cuff and the beginning of the buttonhole must be not less than half the width of the button, otherwise the button would extend beyond the edge. Close the opening and pin through for the button position.

Worked Buttonhole

1) Interline the garment and the facing with organdie and mark out the positions of the buttonholes.
2) Cut the buttonhole along a straight thread, from the outer end towards the inner.
3) Oversew the cut edges with small stitches, catching in the facing which is inclined to slip down.
4) Use buttonhole twist, silk or cotton, whichever is most suitable for the material. One yard of thread will work a buttonhole 1″ long

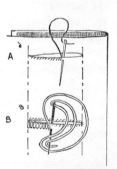

without a join. Beginning with a knot (which can be cut off afterwards) slip the needle between the garment and the facing ½″ away from the inner end of the slit. Bring it out through the slit and work

Buttonhole worked from the front.

buttonhole stitch (see stitches) along the lower edge. The stitches, which should touch each other and be about ⅛" deep, must cover the oversewing.

5) To get round the outer end spread the buttonhole stitches at the base, see C in diagram.

6) Work the stitch along the second side.

7) Put the needle in the knot of the first stitch on the first side bringing it out at the base of the final stitch, see D.

8) Work two stitches across the inner end as at E.

9) Work blanket stitch over the bar thus formed, completely covering it, see F. Fasten off on the W.S.

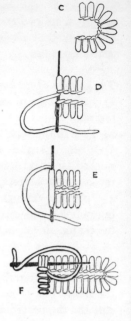

Piped and Bound Buttonholes

1) Back the position with organdie but do not fold the facing under, leave it free. Tack out the buttonholes equal to the diameter of the button plus ⅛".

2) Cut a crossway strip 1½" deep and ¾" longer than the buttonhole. With the R.S. together, place the centre of this strip over the buttonhole mark. Stretch the strip slightly and tack it in position. Machine 1/16" above and below the buttonhole mark and across each end, overlapping four stitches on one side to avoid having to fasten off.

3) Cut through the buttonhole mark from the centre to within ⅛" of each end, then cut diagonally right up to the stitching in each corner.

4) Push the crossway strip through the slit to the W.S.

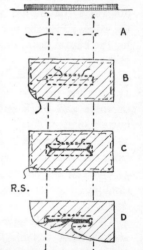

5) For piped buttonholes, press the turnings away from the slit on the W.S. See E in the diagram. For bound buttonholes press them up on to the strip towards the slit, filling it, as at F.

6) Form two even pipings or bindings on the R.S. to fill the slit. On the W.S. inverted pleats will form at each end of the strip. Take a stitch or two across each pleat to hold it.

7) From the R.S. stab stitch round the buttonhole through the seams to hold the piping or binding in place. This is called sink stitching because the stitches sink into the seam and become invisible. Trim down the turnings of the piping to about $\frac{1}{8}''$.

8) Fold the facing of the garment into place on the W.S. and tack through, round each buttonhole, to prevent it slipping, see J.

9) Cut the slit in the facing by putting the scissors through from the R.S.

10) With the point of the needle turn in the raw edges of the slit and hem very strongly to position as the buttonhole gets much wear.

11) For a square finish as at M, cut the slit in the facing to within $\frac{1}{8}''$ of each end and then cut into each corner. Turn in the raw edges and hem in position.

12) Remove the tacking and press under a cloth on the W.S.

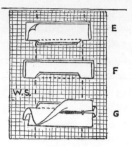

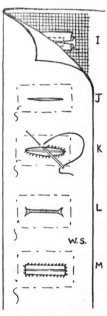

Uses of worked and piped or bound buttonholes
Worked buttonholes are suitable for all garments and materials and have the most tailored appearance. They must be used on transparent materials as piping would show through.

Bound or piped buttonholes are suitable for thicker materials and for those which fray badly. They are particularly useful when the button is large or thick, needing an extra long buttonhole. The piping or binding fills the gap which might otherwise show beyond the end of the button. Piped buttonholes have a sunken and neater appearance than bound ones, which are raised and more conspicuous. However, when material frays badly the bound ones wear better.

Rouleau Loop Buttonholes

Round rouleau is used for buttonloops and flat rouleau for decorative purposes, such as for faggoting, and for convenience both types are described here.

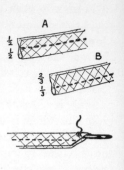

1) *For flat rouleau* cut a crossway strip four times the finished width. Fold in half lengthwise with the R.S. inside and machine through the centre, stretching the material during the stitching. This is important, otherwise the thread will break when the strip is turned out.

2) *For round rouleau* cut the crossway strip six times the finished width and machine two thirds of the folded depth in from the raw edges, stretching it well.

3) *To turn out.* Cut one end to a sharp point. Push a bodkin inside the tube and sew it securely to the point. Turn the rouleau R.S. out over the bodkin.

BUTTONLOOPS

1) From a strip of round rouleau cut off pieces the required length, which can be found by trying it over the button and adding two $\frac{1}{4}''$ turnings.

2) Tack in the fitting line on the garment and make another tack line, the depth of the loops inside it.

3) Tack the loops in position on the R.S. with the rounded ends touching the inner tack line. Arrange the seam to lie on the outside of the rouleau as the loops set better that way. The width of the loops should equal the diameter of the button and they should touch each other.

4) Tack and machine the loops through the fitting line.

5) Place the R.S. of the facing over the loops matching the fitting lines. Tack and machine through the fitting lines.

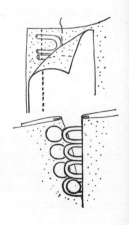

6) Trim the turnings to $\frac{1}{8}''$ or $\frac{1}{4}''$ and turn right side out. This makes the loops extend beyond the edge.

Note. These loops are used when the edges of the opening just meet without overlapping. They look very well when used with buttons covered with the same material.

Worked Buttonloops

Use buttonhole twist, cotton or silk to match the material.

1) Make four stitches on top of each other, quite on the edge of the opening. These stitches must lie flat on the edge and on no account should they loop as they stretch in wear. The length of the stitches equals the diameter of the button, unless this is very thick, when they will have to be a little longer.

2) Work buttonhole stitch over the loops, completely covering them.

3) Sew the buttons on in such a position that when fastened, the edges of the opening just meet.

TO MAKE AN INVISIBLE FASTENING

Make a worked loop $\frac{1}{4}''$ inside the overlapping part of the opening. Sew the button on the underlap to correspond.

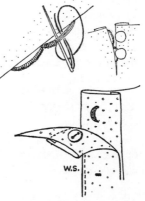

Worked loops are used mainly for underwear and for children's wear.

W.S.

Sewing on Buttons

Some buttons have a shank attached to them to take the thickness of the material round the buttonhole. This type of button is attached with about six over stitches taken through the material and the shank and fastened off securely on the W.S. When a button has no shank, it has to be allowed for during the sewing on.

1) Use buttonhole thread, cotton or silk. Place a pin over the top of the button. Begin on with a knot or backstitch and take four stitches, over the pin, through each hole in the button and through the material.

2) Remove the pin and wind the thread several times round the shank thus formed, making a firm stem.

Take the needle through the material to the W.S. and fasten off with a few over stitches.

Four-hole buttons may be stitched on in the ways illustrated.

Note. If the button has only two holes and the buttonholes are horizontal, they must be stitched on with the holes in a horizontal position to correspond.

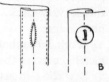

If the buttonholes are vertical, the holes in the button must be placed vertically to match.

A

LINK BUTTONS

These are used, as a rule, to fasten cuffs.

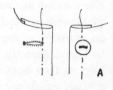

B

1) Connect the buttons with four strands of buttonhole twist leaving the link between the required length.

2) Cover the link completely with buttonhole stitch. To finish off, run the thread back through the stitches.

Press Studs

The part of the press stud with the knob has the flattest base and leaves the least impression when ironed over. For this reason it is sewn on to the top side of the opening. The part with the hole is thicker and is sewn to the underside.

TO SEW ON

Use cotton or silk to match the garment and take four buttonhole stitches through each hole and the material. Pass the thread underneath from one hole to the next. Over stitches may be used, but buttonhole stitches look better and are stronger.

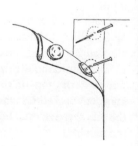

THE POSITION OF PRESS STUDS

The top part of the press stud is stitched on $\frac{1}{8}''$ inside the outer edge of the opening. It is so placed to make it invisible in wear. The distance apart may be from 1″ to 1¼″. Sew all the tops first and press the under parts on to them. Rub chalk over the base of the under pieces and then close the opening and press on the studs. This will give a chalk mark for the position of the under pieces. Pin through these marks as the chalk rubs off.

Hooks and Eyes

These are used for underwear and whenever there may be some strain.

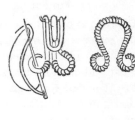

Sew the hooks on with buttonhole stitch covering the loops completely.

Take two or three stitches across the top, inside the hook and through the material.

The wire loop should be entirely covered with buttonhole stitch.

THE POSITION OF HOOKS AND EYES ON A GARMENT

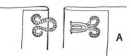

A

a) When the two ends meet, edge to edge, as in the petersham on a skirt, the wire loop type of eye is used.

Sew the hook ⅛″ inside the front edge and sew on the loop to extend ⅛″ beyond the back edge.

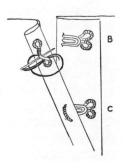

B

C

b) The wire bar is seldom satisfactory in use as it pulls out of shape. It is used for openings which overlap. Sew on the hook ⅛″ in from the top edge of the opening and then close the opening to find the position of the eye. The wire bar is entirely covered with buttonhole stitch.

c) A more durable method is to work the bar with buttonhole twist, silk or cotton by taking four stitches across the position and covering them with buttonhole stitch.

Eyelet Holes

Small eyelet holes are occasionally used to fasten hooks into and larger ones are used to fasten belts with buckles which have latchets.

1) Stitch round the position with tiny running stitches.
2) Punch the hole with a stiletto or a knitting needle.

H

3) Begin with a few running stitches
in the reverse direction and oversew
the edge very tightly, inserting the
stiletto now and again to roll the edge.
4) Buttonhole over the oversewing,
bringing the knotted edge to the inside
of the eyelet.

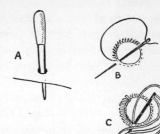

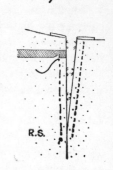

Zip Fasteners

Choose the correct size of fastener for
the material and the position on the
garment. The feather-weight size is suitable for
wrist and neck openings. Light-weight fasteners
may be used for dress and skirt plackets. The
colour of the tape should match that of the garment.

METHOD I

The edges of the opening just meet over the zip
fastener.

1) Press the turnings of the opening under on the
fitting line.

2) Use a marker and make lines of straight tacking $\frac{3}{16}''$ from the edge
on each side of the opening through the garment and the turning.

3) Machine along each tack line, but not across the base.

4) Neaten the edges of the turnings before inserting the zip.

5) Place the right hand side of the opening over the zip so that the
edge lies exactly along the centre of the teeth. Pin in position through
the material and the zip tape, placing the pins about $1''$ apart, as shown.

6) With matching cotton or silk, bring the
needle up in the first machine stitch and
make a stab stitch over this machine stitch.
Miss two machine stitches underneath and
bring the needle through to the R.S. again.
Continue stab stitching, over one stitch on
top and missing two underneath. Fasten off
on the W.S.

7) Pin the second side of the opening to meet
the first, concealing the zip, and stab stitch
through as before.

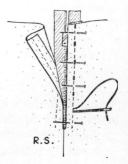

To neaten the base

Oversew the inner edges of the tape together from ¼″ below the teeth. Hem the sides of the tape below the teeth to the seam of the garment. Blanket stitch the raw edges at the base to the seam.

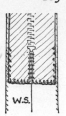

In a dress the top of the zip is treated in the same way, but in a skirt the top tapes are caught into the waistband.

W.S.

METHOD 2

This method conceals the fastener completely.

1) Fold under on the fitting line the turning of the upper edge of the opening. Press and, using a marker, make a line of straight tacking ½″ in from the edge. Machine on this guide line. Fold the under edge of the opening under ⅛″ *OUTSIDE* the fitting line. In order to do this, the turning must be cut across the base as at A, to release the seam. Press and machine along the edge of the fold.

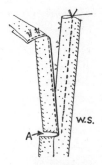

W.S.

A

2) Pin the underside of the opening just to touch the metal teeth of the zip. Stab stitch on to the tape through the line of machining, as for method 1.

3) Pin the upper side over to meet the fitting line of the underside, completely concealing the zip. Stab stitch on through the line of machining and neaten the ends on the W.S. as for method 1.

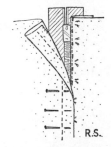

R.S.

Tapes

Tapes are often used as loops for hanging up clothes and household articles, such as towels, ovencloths, etc.

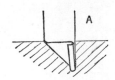

A

SEWING TAPE TO AN EDGE

This method is also suitable for sewing on shoulder straps.

1) Place the tape to the W.S. of the article. The tape must be sewn on in a perfect square, therefore the width of the tape determines how far down on the article it should be placed. This is easily measured by turning in the raw edge and folding

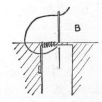

B

the tape back diagonally as in the diagram.
2) Pin the tape to the garment and fold it back
level with the edge. Oversew or seam the edges
together very strongly.
3) Turn the tape up and hem the free edges in
place.

This method can be used for coat and
overall hangers.

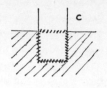

SEWING LOOPS ON THE CORNERS OF HOUSEHOLD ARTICLES

1) Arrange the tape as in the diagram. Fold
up the raw ends and, with a crease, mark off
the depth, equal to twice the width of the
tape as at A. Place the tape in position on the
W.S. of the article with the crease lying
across the corner as at B.

2) Oversew the inner edges of the tape
together from the base as far as the corner
of the article.

3) Hem the lower edges of the tape to the
article on the W.S. and on the R.S. seam the
corner to the tape.

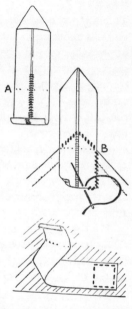

TAPE LOOPS STITCHED FLAT

1) Cut a length of tape and fold the raw ends
under.

Crease the tape to form a perfect square at each end. Place in position
flat on the article.

Tack and machine each end in a square, using the crease as a guide
line.

Belt Carriers

On children's dresses belts are often attached at one side, to avoid
losing them. They are fixed with a small worked link as for linked
buttons. Adult dresses sometimes have belt carriers on the side seams
at the waist. These may be worked with buttonhole twist, as for
worked buttonholes, or they may be made of the same material as the
garment.

METHOD

1) Make a length of flat rouleau. (See under buttonloops.) Cut two strips off the rouleau, each 1″ longer than the width of the belt.

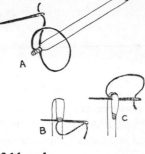

A

2) Fasten a length of cotton to each end and twist it tightly round the end to neaten it and to draw it in. See A in diagram.

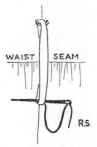

B   C

3) Fold the ends over ¼″ as at B and stitch them to the carrier.

4) Slip the needle under the top of the fold and take two or three stitches round it to prevent the rouleau spreading out, as at C.

5) Place the carrier in position on the side seam of the garment with the waist seam in the centre of it.

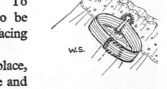

WAIST   SEAM

R.S.

Stitch it to the garment through the folded loop at each end.

Elastic in Knickers

Make a worked buttonhole in the top facing of the knickers before fixing it down. To strengthen it, the position will have to be backed with a piece of organdie, as the facing is single material.

W.S.

When the casing has been stitched in place, thread the elastic through the buttonhole and overlap the ends for ¼″. Blanket stitch over the raw ends of the elastic and oversew the sides together, then let it slip back inside the casing.

XIII: Pockets

Patch Pockets

These are used a lot in needlework and before they can be applied the top hem and any corners must be dealt with.

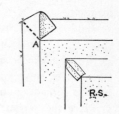

1) When the material is thick, fold the hem and the side turnings on to the R.S. on the fitting lines. Nip up the corners so that the edges of the hem and turnings meet as at A. Stitch together from A to the corner. Trim off the corner and press the seam open. Turn the hem to the W.S. and fix with Paris binding or herringbone stitch.

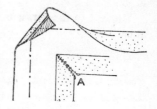

2) For thin materials, fold the corners across on the W.S. at such an angle that when the hem and side seams are turned over on the fitting lines, the edges will meet at A. The angle of the first fold depends on the depth of the hem.

3) When a hem has been stitched before the corner has been treated, fold the top corners over as in the diagram, to the W.S. and then fold the side turnings over. Tack in position.

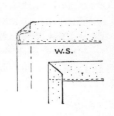

4) In this example the pocket has a shaped facing on the R.S. Place the R.S. of the facing to the W.S. of the pocket. Tack and stitch the fitting lines together from A, round the top to A. Trim the turnings to $\frac{1}{8}''$ and cut the corners as the diagram shows. Turn the facing over to the R.S. Turn in the lower edge and tack and machine in place.

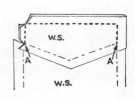

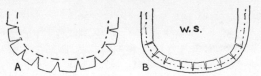

Treating a rounded base of a pocket
Cut wedge shaped pieces out of the turnings,
round the curve, so that they will set flat when
turned over on the fitting lines and tacked.

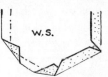

A pointed base
On the W.S. fold the turnings across the
point of each corner. Then fold all turnings
over on the fitting line, tack and press.

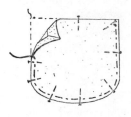

Attaching the pocket
Place the pocket on the R.S. of the garment
matching the fitting lines. Pin across the
corners securely. Tack in position and
machine round the edge.

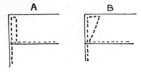

To strengthen the top corners
1) Machine in either of the ways illustrated above.
2) Hem a small square of Paris binding behind the corner and work a
tailors' catch through it. (See stitches.)

Thin Bound Pocket

If the pocket is used in wear, it should measure 5″ across and 5½″
deep. A breast pocket may be 3″–3½″ long.
1) With a tack line mark the position of the pocket opening on the
R.S. of the garment.
2) Cut a piece of material for the pocket on the straight grain, the
required width of the pocket plus 1″, for turnings, by twice the depth
plus 1¼″.

3) Find the centre of this pocket piece and make a tack line $\frac{1}{2}''$ below it to mark the position of the opening.

4) With the right sides together, place the tack line of the pocket piece over the tack line on the garment, making sure that the deeper part of the pocket piece lies above it. Tack together.

5) Machine round the tack line, $\frac{1}{4}''$ above and below it and across each end. Overlap the stitching for $\frac{1}{2}''$ to avoid having to fasten off.

6) Cut through the tack line from the centre to within $\frac{1}{4}''$ of each end and then cut quite into each corner as for a buttonhole.

7) Push the pocket piece through the slit to the W.S. and press each seam towards the opening.

8) Fold the pocket pieces up and down over the turnings, enclosing them to form an even binding on the R.S. On the W.S. pull the pocket piece at each end to make inverted pleats.

9) Sink stitch from the R.S. through the seams, to hold the binding in place, as for a buttonhole.

10) Turn to the W.S. and fold the top part of the pocket down over the lower part. Pin and tack together to make the pocket bag. Machine through the fitting lines with the garment uppermost and the pocket down on the machine plate. This is important in order to catch in the triangular piece at each top corner. Make the corners round at the base to prevent the accumulation of fluff and dust, during wear.

11) Trim the turnings to $\frac{1}{2}''$ and neaten them by blanket stitching together. Alternatively they may be bound with crossway material.

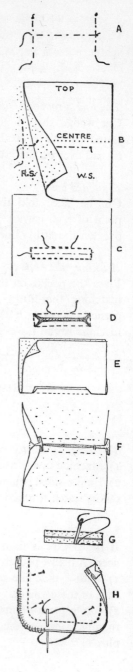

Pocket Cut as Part of the Garment

This type of pocket may be found in shorts, slacks and skirts. Sometimes, variations of it may be used on blouses and pyjama jackets.

1) The position of the edge of the pocket is marked on the underlay piece with a line of tacking.

2) Place the R.S. of the facing to the R.S. of the garment. Tack and stitch the fitting lines together. If the seam is curved snip across the turnings to the stitching. Trim the turnings to $\frac{1}{8}''$.

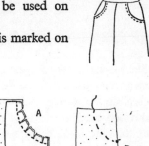

3) Press down the turnings on the facing only, to bring the seam to the inside when turned out.

4) Turn the facing completely to the W.S. and tack along the edge to keep the seam in place.

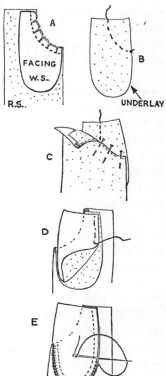

5) With the right sides uppermost, lap the faced part over the underlay matching the edge to the tack line. Pin and tack.

6) On the W.S. pin and tack the underlay to the pocket facing to form the bag. Make sure this sets absolutely flat.

7) Machine the underlay and the facing together through the fitting lines.

8) Trim the turnings to $\frac{1}{2}''$ and neaten with blanket stitch, oversewing or crossway binding, whichever method suits the rest of the garment.

XIV: Sleeves

Sleeves are a very important part of a garment and must be made up and set in carefully. Usually they are completely finished before being put into the armhole as they are more easily handled when they are unattached.

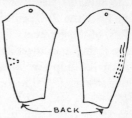

BACK

PAIRING SLEEVES

There is a left and a right sleeve to a garment and it is easy to tell which is which by observing the following points.

1) The back of a tight sleeve is longer than the front and is eased in at the elbow for comfort in wear. This extra length may be taken out in darts or gathers.

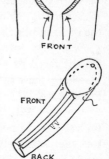

FRONT

FRONT

BACK

2) The back of a sleeve dips at the wrist to allow for it to be taken up when the arm is bent.

3) When the sleeve is folded in half the head is slightly deeper at the back to allow for movement.

MAKING THE SLEEVE UP

1) Pin the sleeve seam together at the wrist and the armhole. Adjust the extra amount at the back at the elbow. Note that darts at the elbow are pressed downwards. Make the darts first and then machine the seam and press open. Neaten the edges.

2) Run a gathering thread round the head of the sleeve through the fitting line from about 3″ either side of the underarm seam.

Setting a Plain Sleeve into the Armhole

1) Trim the turnings of the sleeve and armhole to $\frac{1}{2}$″.

2) With the R.S. outside, pin the centre top of the sleeve to the shoulder seam of the garment. Ease the sleeve $2\frac{1}{2}$″–3″ either side of this pin and pin to the armhole as in the diagram. The sleeve is cut 1″–$1\frac{1}{2}$″ larger than the armhole so that it may fit comfortably

over the top of the shoulder and the extra
amount is eased in here. It must not pleat nor
look gathered in any way.

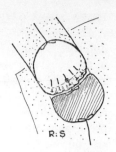

3) Place a hand under the shoulder seam to
make sure the sleeve hangs correctly. It
should hang slightly forward with the grain of
the material running from the top of the
shoulder to the little finger.

4) Turn to the W.S. and pin the rest of the
sleeve into the armhole, stretching it slightly
at the back from A to B. The sleeve seam
may lie on the garment seam, or it may be ¾"
to the front of it.

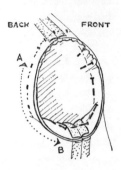

Commercial patterns are usually seam to
seam and they have notches on both sleeve
and armhole which must be matched when
the sleeve is pinned in.

5) Pull up the gathering thread until the
sleeve fits the armhole. With the *SLEEVE
HELD UPPERMOST*, tack in place through
the fitting lines rolling it over the hand to
disperse the fullness at the top. Tack with
small stitches. If the material is woollen, the
fullness may be shrunk away under a damp
cloth with a hot iron.

6) Beginning 1" away from the underarm
seam, machine through the fitting lines with
the sleeve uppermost and the garment down
on the machine. Finish the stitching 1" beyond the underarm seam so
that it overlaps 2" at this part which takes the most strain in wear.

7) Trim the turnings and neaten them together.

8) Press under a cloth on the W.S. using a sleeve pad. See 'Pressing'.
Press out any fullness at the top and press the seam towards the sleeve.

Finding the position of a wrist opening
Fold the sleeve into four. The fold next to
the back of the sleeve is the position for
the opening, when the sleeve is gathered
into a cuff or has a tightly fitting wrist.

When it is convenient the opening may be made in the seam.

INSERTING OTHER TYPES OF SLEEVE

Apart from the plain sleeve there are other types of sleeve needing different treatment. Puff sleeves with a gathered head are inserted in the same way as plain sleeves except that the fullness is allowed to remain and is usually arranged over the shoulder from about 3″ either side of the shoulder seam. Shirt sleeves are used for shirts, pyjamas and shirt blouses. Magyar or kimono sleeves are cut in one with the bodice and sometimes have a diamond shaped gusset inserted under the arm for ease and comfort in wear. The raglan type is used on dresses, blouses, dressing gowns, overalls and jackets. It comes and goes in fashion.

Shirt Sleeve

1) Use a double stitched seam to sew up the shoulder seams of the garment. Leave the side seams un-stitched.
2) With the R.S. outside, pin and tack the sleeve into the armhole, easing the fullness over the shoulder.
3) Fix with a double stitched seam.
4) Join the underarm and side seams with double stitched seams, from the wrist to the hem, making sure the ends of the armhole seam meet under the arm.

Magyar or Kimono Sleeve

1) The sleeve is stitched with a plain seam, all in one with the side seam of the garment.
2) Snip the turnings across to the stitching at the underarm where the seam is curved, for comfort in wear. This weakens the seam, and, to avoid the material splitting, cut a crossway strip 1″ wide and long enough to cover the clipped part. Turn in each raw end and hem it across the turnings as in the diagram. Neaten the sides of the strip in with the turnings. This method is suitable

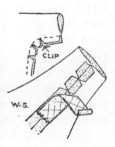

when the sleeve is loose, but, when it fits more tightly, it may be uncomfortable unless a gusset is inserted.

Inserting a gusset into a magyar sleeve
The gusset is inserted into slits cut in the garment at the underarm.
1) Mark the position of the slit, 4″ long, with tacking.
2) Cut a crossway strip 1¼″ wide, from thin material such as taffeta. Place the centre of it over the tack line on the W.S. of the garment and tack through.
3) Machine ⅛″ either side of the tack line tapering *BLUNTLY* to a point at the top.
4) Cut through the tack line quite up to the top stitch.
5) Fold the crossway strip over on the line of stitching and press it towards the slit.
6) For the gusset, cut a triangular piece of material with the sides 4½″ long and the base about 4″ across. These measurements include turnings.
7) Place the R.S. of the gusset into the R.S. of the slit. Allow ¼″ turnings on the gusset and tack and machine it to the garment only, immediately inside and along the fold of the crossway strip.
8) Trim the turnings of the strip to ¼″ level with those of the gusset. Neaten them together with blanket stitch.
9) Treat both the back and front of the garment in this way and then tack up and machine the side and underarm seam.
Note. A nicer method is to insert one diamond shaped gusset instead of the two triangular ones. Make the slits in the back and front as above, then stitch the side and underarm seams of the garment, without catching in the crossway strip. The gusset is then inserted and finished as above.

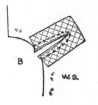
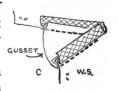
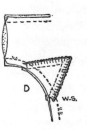

Raglan Sleeve

1) Stitch the dart in the head of the sleeve.
2) Pin, tack and stitch the back and front armhole seams of the sleeve to the bodice. These seams are usually curved and must be snipped

across to the stitch-
ing so that they may
be pressed out flat.
Trim and neaten
them.

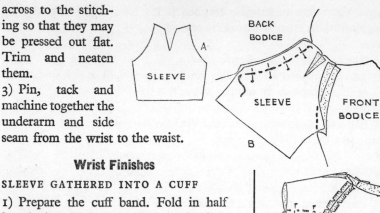

3) Pin, tack and
machine together the
underarm and side
seam from the wrist to the waist.

Wrist Finishes

SLEEVE GATHERED INTO A CUFF

1) Prepare the cuff band. Fold in half
lengthwise, W.S. out. Tack and stitch
the ends from the fold to the fitting line
only, as at A in the diagram, leaving the
turnings free.

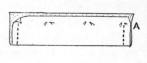

2) Trim the stitched turnings to $\frac{1}{8}''$ and
turn the band R.S. out. Tack through at
each end and along the folded edge. Fold
one turning only, in on the fitting line and
tack it.

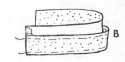

3) Complete the sleeve opening. Run
two gathering threads round the sleeve,
$\frac{1}{8}''$ apart, either side of the fitting line.
Leave the space A in the diagram from
the underlap of the opening to the seam
ungathered. Pull up the threads until the
sleeve fits the band.

4) Place the cuff to the W.S. of the sleeve
and pin in position distributing the gathering evenly. Tack and machine between
the two
gathering
threads.

5) Trim
the turn-
ings to $\frac{1}{4}''$
and turn
the cuff

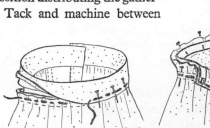

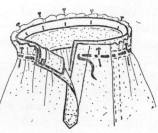

up. Tack the turnings to it. Pin and tack
the free folded edge of the cuff to cover the
machining.

6) Machine all round the cuff.

7) Fasten with buttons and buttonholes.

Note. This cuff may be stitched to the R.S.
of the sleeve in stage 4 and hemmed on the
W.S. in stage 6, so that no machine stitching
will show on the R.S.

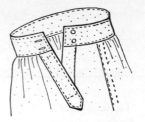

TURN BACK CUFF

Method 1

1) Prepare the cuff and tack one of the
turnings, as at A, $\frac{1}{16}$" inside the fitting line,
thus making the side slightly shorter than
the other one.

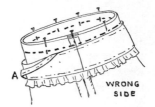

2) Place the unfolded edge of the cuff to the
W.S. of the sleeve, seam to seam. Pin, tack
and stitch together through the fitting lines.

3) Turn the sleeve R.S. out. Turn the cuff
away from the sleeve and press the turnings
up on to it.

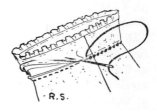

4) Pin and tack the free folded edge of the
cuff to the machine stitching and hem it
down. When the cuff is turned back the
hemming will not show.

Method 2. This is used for thicker material
and when the cuff does not form a continuous band.

1) Pin, tack and machine the cuff in place
on the R.S. of the sleeve, through all
thicknesses.

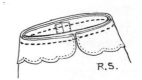

2) Turn to the W.S. and turn the cuff down
and the turnings up on to the sleeve. Trim
down the inner turnings and tack the outer
one to the sleeve.

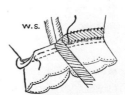

3) Cover the raw edge with Paris or crossway binding and hem both sides to position.

XV: Belts and Waistbands

There are two main types of belt, the mitred kind fastening with buckles or hooks, and the tie belt. The former may be stiffened but the latter seldom are.

Mitred Belt

1) Fold the belt in half lengthwise with the R.S. inside. Tack and stitch the fitting lines together but not across the ends. Trim the turnings to $\frac{1}{8}''$.

2) Press the seam open and arrange it to lie down the centre of the belt.

3) To make the point or mitre, put a tack line AB across one end and make another tack line CD half the width of the belt away from it. Make tack lines from C and D crossing in the centre of the AB line.

4) Stitch the point along the tack lines and trim the turnings to $\frac{1}{8}''$ cutting them off across the point.

5) Push the point into the belt with the end of a pencil and turn right side out over it.

6) Arrange the seam down the centre of the underside. Tack round the edges and press.

7) Fasten with a buckle or with two hooks and a press stud at the point.

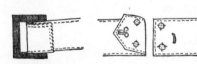

MITRED BELT STIFFENED

Canvas, organdie, petersham or adhesive belt stiffening may be used for the interlining.

1) Cut the interlining the exact width and length of the belt. The

length is usually the waist measure plus 4″–5″ for the wrap over. Cut the mitre at one end as described for the mitred belt.

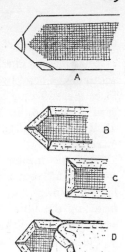

2) In this case the belt is made from two separate pieces of material. Place the interlining to the W.S. of one piece and fold the turnings over it on the fitting lines. Tack in place and catch stitch the raw edges to the stiffening, unless the interlining is adhesive, when it is ironed on, and the catch stitching is unnecessary.

3) On the second piece of material fold the turnings under on the fitting lines and tack them and press. Place this over the interlining on the belt and tack through. Slip stitch the two edges together all round or machine them, as desired.

Tie Belt

This is a long soft belt used on dresses (particularly children's), aprons and on dressing-gowns.

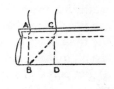

1) Fold the belt in half lengthwise with the W.S. outside. Mark the points at each end by making a tack line AB across the end and then another one CD the whole width of the belt away from it. Make a tack line from C to B. The point is stitched along this CB line.

2) Tack and stitch the ends and the length but leave 2″ unstitched in the centre in order that the ends may be turned out through this opening later.

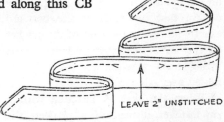

LEAVE 2″ UNSTITCHED

3) Trim the turnings to ⅛″ and cut them off at an angle at the points to enable them to turn out sharply.

4) Turn each end out, over a pencil, through the opening in the centre. Slip stitch the edges of the opening together. Tack round the edges and press.

I

Waistband Attached to a Skirt

PREPARATION OF THE BAND

1) Cut a piece of interlining the exact finished width of the band by the whole length of it. Place this stiffening to the W.S. of the band level with the fitting lines as in the diagram. Tack and fix in place with a zig-zag line of machining.

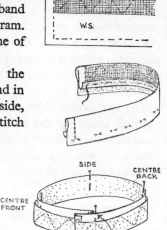

2) Fold the turning of the band over the stiffening and tack in place. Fold the band in half lengthwise with the W.S. outside, matching the fitting lines. Tack and stitch across each end. Trim turnings to $\frac{1}{8}''$.

3) Put a pin in the band at the beginning of the underlap extension. This is the position of the left side seam of the skirt. Place the other end to touch this pin and fold the band in half. Put a pin $\frac{1}{2}''$ away from this fold on the side which has the extension. This makes the back of the band 1″ shorter than the front. This pin is the position of the right side seam. Place pins in the centre back and centre front of the waistband.

4) Put pins at the centre front and back of the skirt. Place the R.S. of the band to the R.S. of the skirt matching the pins on the band to those on the skirt. Make certain that the ends of the belt are exactly flush with the ends of the placket on the skirt. Pin, tack and stitch the fitting lines together, level with the folded over edge of the band.

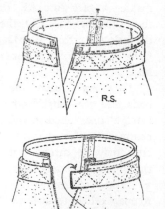

5) When the skirt is fastened with a zip fastener instead of a placket, the extension part or underlapon the band must be stitched and turned out before the band is tacked to the skirt. *Note* that the front end of the band is placed flush with the end of the skirt and at

the back the underlap extends beyond the zip. This extension is held in place with a hook and eye.

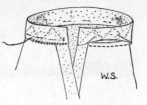

6) Trim the turnings to $\frac{1}{4}''$ and press them up on to the band. Place the free folded edge of the band over the stitching and tack and hem it in place.

Note. If machining on the R.S. is required, the band is placed to the W.S. of the skirt in stage 4 and is turned over to the R.S. and machined in place.

XVI: Repairs

Darning

Darning is suitable for repairing small holes and thin places in knitted and woven fabrics. Use a long fine darning needle and thread which matches the article as nearly as possible in colour and thickness. Use flax for linen materials, cotton for cotton and silk for silk. For woollen material use ravellings from the seams or fine mending wool.

In knitted goods the darning is usually worked on the W.S. but on material which is woven it is easier to work on the R.S.

DARNING A THIN PLACE ON WOVEN MATERIAL

1) Darn along the selvedge threads, as this is the way the material is woven. Begin well outside the thin place so that all the weak parts may be completely covered.

2) Make small running stitches through the material, the length of the stitches equalling the spaces between—on coarse material the threads may be counted. The distance apart of the rows of stitching should equal the length of the stitch. At the end of each row leave a small loop about $\frac{1}{8}''$ deep to allow the darning thread to shrink when laundered.

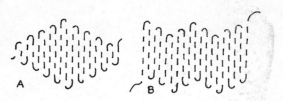

3) To avoid the strain coming all on one thread, darns should not be straight along the top or base. The shape should be graduated as illustrated.

DARNING A HOLE IN WOVEN MATERIAL

1) Begin well outside the hole and any surrounding thin part and darn through the material as for a thin place, carrying the thread across the hole.

2) Turn the work and beginning outside
the hole, darn across, taking the needle
alternately over and under the previous
stitches and through the fabric.

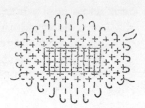

DARN FOR A CROSS CUT

This is a clean slit cut on the cross.

1) Outline the shape of the darn with
tacking as in the diagram. ABCD is
a square, B and C are $\frac{1}{4}''$ away from the
ends of the slit. BE and CF equal AB.
Tack in the shape AEFD. Turn the
work round and tack the same shape
across.

2) Darn the upright selvedge way first.

3) Turn the work and darn the weft
way making a zig-zag pattern where
the stitches cross.

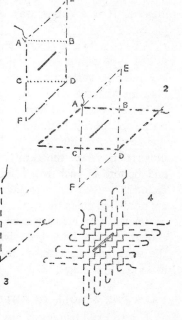

DARNING A HEDGE
OR CORNER TEAR

This is usually
caused by catching a
garment on some-
thing sharp and the
result is a right-
angled tear along the
threads. There is no
surrounding   weak
part so the darn may be worked along
straight threads.

1) It is helpful to draw the edges together
with fish-bone stitch by taking the needle
through under one
side of the slit and
then through under
the other.

2) Begin the weft
way about $\frac{1}{2}''$ outside the tear and

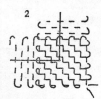

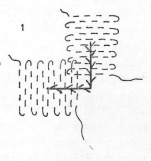

darn across until a little more than three-quarters of the way up the slit. Leave the thread hanging.

3) Turn the work and repeat across the selvedge way.

4) Turn again and finish darning the weft way.

5) Complete the selvedge darning, making a pattern where the stitches cross.

MACHINE DARNING

This is a very suitable method for the repair of household linen and lingerie. It is a strong way of mending slits, small holes and thin places.

1) A darning foot can be attached to the sewing machine and, according to the type of machine, the part which feeds the work through is lowered or covered with a plate to put it out of action. Thread up the machine with the special fine cotton made for the purpose.

2) Fix the part to be darned into an embroidery frame and pass it backwards and forwards under the needle forming rows of stitching as in the illustration. Make the turning points at the top and bottom of each row blunt. Machine darning can only be satisfactorily worked on a treadle or an electric machine as both hands are needed to guide the work. When an edge wears, as it does frequently on towels, darn across the worn part moving the frame rapidly, until enough threads have been worked across the space to fill it. Turn the work and darn across these threads making a firm edge.

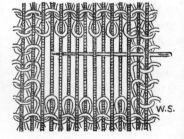

DARN FOR A HOLE IN KNITTED FABRIC

1) Unravel and trim away any fraying threads making the hole oblong or square.

2) Work on the W.S. The stitches in plain knitting run in rows of loops which link together. This is clearly seen on the W.S. Beginning at the bottom left hand corner, thread the needle alternately over and under these loops. Each loose loop at the top and bottom of the hole is opposite a space. Always pass the thread through these loops from underneath, as this keeps the R.S. tidy. Be careful to keep

the correct sequence of over and under stitches and leave $\frac{1}{8}''$ loops at the end of each row. Graduate the shape as illustrated.

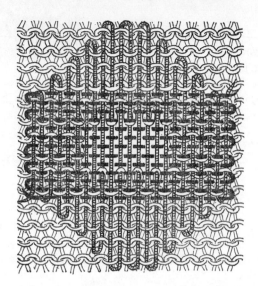

3) Turn the work round and darn across the hole from well outside it. One row of darning comes between the rows of knitted loops and the next one is worked on the loops where they link together, and so on.

SWISS DARNING

This is an invisible way of strengthening a thin place in coarsely knitted fabric, such as the elbows of cardigans. If possible use the same wool from which the garment was made.

1) Work this darn on the R.S. from the right to the left. Use a piece of wool as long as is conveniently possible.

2) Begin on the W.S. by running the wool through a few stitches and then bring the needle through to the R.S. just outside the worn part.

3) Follow the knitting stitch by passing the needle under a loop in one row and then under the next loop along in the row above.

4) To turn the corner, turn the work

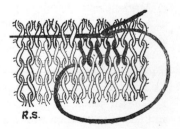

R.S.

upside down and follow the diagram. To
end off run the wool through a few stitches
on the W.S.

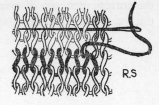

Patching

Keep the good parts of worn out linen
and clothing for patching. There is less
strain on the article or garment if the patch is not of new material.
If the material must be new it should be well washed before being
applied in case it shrinks.

GENERAL RULES

1) The patch must match the article as nearly as possible in weave and
colour.
2) All patches must be cut on the same grain as the part to be patched.
3) Linen should be patched before laundering to prevent further
damage.
4) Print and cloth patches are placed on the R.S. of garments and
those on household linen and on garments worn next to the skin are
put on the W.S.
5) Patches may be square or oblong and must cover all the surrounding
weak part.

MACHINE DARNED PATCHES

This type of patch is very suitable for household linen and lingerie.

Patch for linen
1) Cut the patch $\frac{3}{8}''$ larger all
round than the hole.
2) Tack it in position on the W.S.
Make a tack line on the patch
outlining the hole to act as a guide.
3) Machine darn round the patch
to a depth of $\frac{5}{8}''$ so that the stitching is
carried $\frac{1}{8}''$ beyond each raw edge.

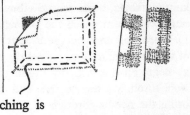

Fitted patch for lingerie
1) Tack net to the W.S. behind the hole.
2) Cut the patch the exact size of the hole
and tack it in position to the net.

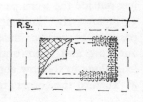

3) Machine darn across the raw edges to a depth of $\frac{3}{8}''$. Cut the net away at the back.

FITTED PATCH FOR A SKIN GLOVE

When patching leather a rather different method must be used to prevent it splitting.

1) Cut the patch from an old glove, the exact size of the hole, making it oval or round.

2) Work buttonhole stitch round the edge of both the patch and the hole, with the knot of the stitch lying on the edge.

3) Fit the patch in place and oversew the knots of the buttonhole stitches together very closely.

PRINT PATCH

This patch is used to repair thin printed material.

1) Cut the patch large enough to cover all the worn part and allow $\frac{1}{2}''$ turnings all round. The grain and the pattern must match that of the garment exactly.

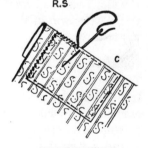

2) Fold the turnings under and crease the edge. Unfold them and cut off the corners $\frac{1}{8}''$ outside the crease, then fold them back again making the corners sharp as in the diagram.

3) Pin the patch in place on the R.S. matching the pattern everywhere. Tack in position.

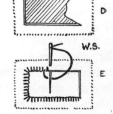

4) Fold the garment over, level with one edge of the patch, along the selvedge threads. Use fine cotton and seam the edges together very closely by taking up one thread only from the garment and one from the patch. Stitch along each side in this way.

5) On the W.S. trim the turnings to $\frac{3}{8}''$ and neaten them together with blanket stitch.

K

CALICO PATCH

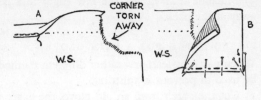

The calico patch is used for mending aprons, overalls and most household linen. The diagrams show how to repair the torn corner of a sheet or tablecloth.

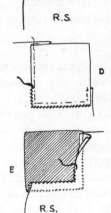

1) Unpick part of the hem.

2) Cut a patch the required size plus $\frac{1}{2}''$ turnings all round, unless a piece with a selvedge edge can be used, in which case no turning need be allowed on the selvedge side.

3) Turn the raw edges of the patch under $\frac{1}{8}''$ and place it to the W.S. of the sheet, matching the selvedge and weft threads exactly. Pin and tack.

4) Hem the two inner edges of the patch to the sheet and remove the tacking.

5) Turn to the R.S. and trim away the torn part of the sheet, leaving $\frac{1}{4}''$ turnings.

6) Fold the raw edges in $\frac{1}{8}''$. (To do this the corner must be snipped into for $\frac{1}{8}''$.) This makes a hem $\frac{3}{8}''$ wide. Tack and hem it in place.

7) Fold the hem of the sheet in position again and re-stitch it.

FLANNEL PATCH

The patch is used for flannel and knitted fabrics, such as stockinet. It is a very flat patch which makes it suitable for underwear. The example illustrated is a baby's vest worn under the arm.

1) Unpick the armhole facing and part of the side seam.

2) Cut a flannel patch on the same grain as the garment and large enough to cover the worn part with $\frac{1}{2}''$ turnings all round.

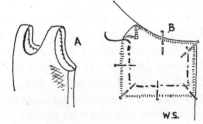

3) As the vest is worn next to the skin, pin the patch over the worn part on the W.S. matching the selvedge and weft threads exactly. (When the fabric is knitted, the rows

of knitting must be matched.) Tack in place.

4) Herringbone the raw edges to the garment, making the lower part of the stitch touch the edge of the patch. Note, in the diagram, how the stitch crosses the corner.

5) Cut away the worn part leaving turnings twice the depth of the herringbone stitch.

6) Herringbone these raw edges to the patch.

7) Sew up the side seams of the garment and re-face the armhole.

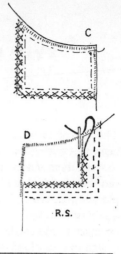

CLOTH PATCH

The cloth patch is suitable for flannel trousers and for corduroy.

1) Outline the shape of the patch, with tacking, on the garment.

2) Cut away the worn part making the hole square or oblong. Snip diagon-ally into each corner as far as the tacking.

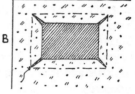

3) Tack the outline of the hole on to the patch and cut the patch out with $\frac{1}{4}$″ turnings. Make sure the grain and nap match the garment. Cut off the corners of the turnings to avoid bulk and then fold them under on the tack line, to the W.S.

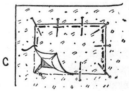

4) Place the patch on the R.S. of the gar-ment matching the grain and the tack lines. Pin across and tack in position.

5) Slip tack the edges of the patch through the fold to the garment. (See Slip Tacking.)

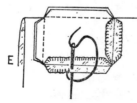

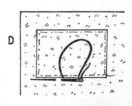

6) Remove the first tacking holding the patch in place. Turn to the W.S. and machine the seams along the slip tacking. Make the corners strong.

7) Press the seams open and neaten them with blanket stitch.

XVII: Embroidery Design and Preparation

The use of embroidery transfers is very unenterprising and nowhere near so exciting as designing one's own patterns and planning how to work them out in embroidery stitches. Very simple everyday articles can be sketched and arranged in many interesting ways to make pleasing patterns. The illustration shows a decorative way of treating a box of matches and a lighted candle in a window—all of them very ordinary things made into a design. Look for design in everything—a group of leaves stuck on a wet pavement, umbrellas, garden tools flung down on the grass and so on. All these things can form the basis for interesting design. Keep on experimenting with different materials and if you want to sew on sequins and beads and buttons and braid to produce some special effect then by all means do it. Break away from convention and be original.

CUT PAPER SHAPES

Arranging shapes cut from paper is a simple way of making patterns. Fold up small pieces of paper several times, snip round them and cut pieces out of them, then open them out to see if the result is interesting enough to be built up into an embroidery design. Shapes can be cut from gummed

coloured paper, from patterned wall paper or from material and arranged on a background sheet of paper. In this way colour, texture and design can be planned at the same time. When the arrangement is satisfactory the shapes can be gummed down or pencilled round onto the background sheet.

The illustration shows a single unit, two motifs for lingerie, two borders and a design suitable for quilting, all of them built up from cut paper shapes of crescents, stars and circles.

GROUPING STITCHES

Borders for tray cloths, aprons, curtains and so on may be built up by arranging and grouping simple embroidery stitches. A few suggestions are given in the diagram: (a) consists of two rows of blanket stitch facing each other, interlaced with a thread of a different colour; (b) is a row of three-cornered loop stitch

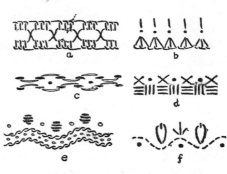

topped by French knots and single straight stitches; (c) two rows of large running stitches interlaced with threads of a different colour and French knots between; (d) shows groups of three straight stitches, alternately horizontal and upright, topped by cross stitches alternating with French knots; (e) is made up of stem stitch, satin stitch and French knots while (f) consists of lazy daisy stitch, straight stitches, backstitch and French knots.

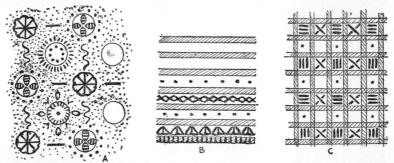

DESIGNING ON PATTERNED MATERIALS

The examples given show how to build up embroidery patterns

on printed or woven materials such as a striped, check or spotted material.

METHODS OF TRANSFERRING THE DESIGN ON TO MATERIAL

The next problem is to outline the design on the material and there are several ways of doing it.

1) Pencil or chalk round cut paper shapes. If chalk is used the pattern must be tacked round later with small stitches otherwise it will rub off.

2) Trace the design onto cartridge paper and place it, right side up, on a piece of ironing board felt. Fix the eye end of a long darning needle into a large cork and, using this, prick through the paper all round the design spacing the perforations $\frac{1}{8}''$ to $\frac{1}{4}''$ apart, depending on how complicated the pattern is. On the underside of the paper the pricks will appear as small bumps and it is most important to smooth these down with fine sandpaper. The design is then placed in position, right side up, on the right side of the material and pinned securely all round. Obtain a small velvet pad (a shoe polishing pad is ideal) and some powdered charcoal from a chemist. Dip the pad in the charcoal and rub it lightly all over the design, taking care not to carry it beyond the edge of the paper as the charcoal is messy. Lift off the paper very carefully and the design will show on the material in small black spots. The pattern must now be outlined with a suitable water colour paint and a fairly dry paint brush to prevent the paint spreading. After painting shake off the charcoal.

3) Wipe over the surface of a piece of carbon paper so that it will not smudge and place it, right side down, onto the right side of the material. Pin the pattern on top, placing the pins immediately outside the carbon paper, otherwise the pin marks will show. With a hard pencil trace the pattern through. This method is the least desirable of all because however careful one is, carbon paper does smudge and is not always easy to wash out. It is only recommended for use on material which does not take water colour satisfactorily.

4) When the material is transparent, designs may be traced directly through with pencil or paint.

5) Sometimes it is not desirable that pencilled or painted lines should be made, particularly on delicate lingerie. In this case trace the pattern on to strong tissue paper and tack it, right side up, in position on the material. Use silk or cotton of a matching colour and trace the outline with tiny running stitches taken through the paper and the material. Tear away the paper very carefully.

Types of Embroidery

I. APPLIQUÉ

This is often used on children's clothes, aprons and household articles. Materials of contrasting colours and textures are applied with embroidery stitches to the background material.

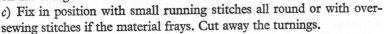

a) Trace the design on to the background and also on to the material which is to be applied.

b) Cut out the shapes of the applied pieces allowing ¼″ turnings all round. Arrange them in place on the background.

c) Fix in position with small running stitches all round or with oversewing stitches if the material frays. Cut away the turnings.

d) Outline with suitable embroidery stitches, completely covering the raw edges. Very close blanket stitch, satin, punch or pin stitches may be used.

Very exciting effects can be obtained in appliqué with the use of different textured materials. It gives great scope for experiment and originality. The illustration shows a picture designed for appliqué of a girl gathering apples. The background could be blue linen and the grass in the foreground applied brushed rayon in green. The girl's dress could be either attractively striped material or plain cotton with the stripes embroidered onto it. The overskirt might be broderie Anglaise. The basket would look well in small checked tweed or even plastic with a handle of twisted cord stitched on. Use a shiny material for the apples or embroider them, dull pink rayon for the flesh, felt for the leaves and flowers and yellow net for the sun rays. Shoes and belt are worked in satin stitch and the hair in stem stitch.

2. SHADOW WORK

Shadow work is used to decorate fine linen blouses, tablecloths and runners, duchess sets and so on. Very delicate shadow effects are obtained by working double backstitch on the wrong side of transparent materials. The most suitable materials for the work are organdie, very fine linen, nylon and terylene. The material must be fine enough for the stitch to show through to give the shadow effect. When coloured embroidery threads are used the colour glows faintly through the material, giving a very attractive appearance.

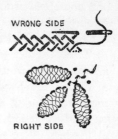

Double backstitch consists of two parallel rows of backstitch worked with the same thread. Take a backstitch in the lower row and then one immediately above in the upper row. Continue in this way crossing the thread between each stitch, see diagram. On the one side it looks like two rows of backstitch and on the reverse side like a double herringbone. For shadow work the stitch is worked on the underside giving a backstitch outline on the right side.

3. RICHELIEU

The design is outlined with running stitches or a cord over which loop stitch is worked very closely with the looped edge towards the part which is to be cut away. See diagram. The veins of the leaves are bars of silk covered with loop stitch which is not worked through the material. When working out designs for this type of work the parts which are cut away must not be too large or the pattern will be untidy and not very hard wearing. This type of work is frequently used to finish the raw edges of table linen.

4. ENGLISH QUILTING

Used for padding cot quilts and dressing-gowns to give warmth. This is worked through three layers of material, the underneath one is

muslin, the middle one may be domette or pre-shrunk flannel or even wadding, and the top one is the outside material.

Place the three layers on top of each other flat on the table and baste tack them together all over very thoroughly.

The design is outlined on the top layer and the quilting is carried out by stab stitching through the outline. When a large article is being worked it is most easily done if the edges are oversewn to a wooden frame. When cot quilts are made the under lining material replaces the layer of muslin so that the design may show on both sides of the quilt.

English quilting may be carried out very successfully with the sewing machine using the special quilting foot.

5. ITALIAN QUILTING

Used to decorate collars, dressing jackets, nightdress sachets and so on.

a) Tack a layer of muslin to the wrong side of the material and pencil the pattern on the muslin.

b) Outline the design through both layers of material with fine running stitches or with machine stitching.

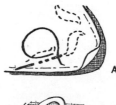

c) On the wrong side run quilting wool between the muslin and the material inside the pattern, thus raising it. When transparent materials are used very brightly coloured wool may be inserted and it will show through in an attractive way.

MAKING UP ARTICLES

Bedspreads can be made from embroidered panels joined together. The sides of the panels are turned in and loop stitched and they are then connected to each other by lacing the looped edges together. Alternatively the edges can be joined with faggoting.

To fit smoothly cushion covers should be 1″ larger than the cushion. The edges may be finished with inserted frills or by piping with crossway material folded over piping cord. The cord must be washed

before use as it shrinks. An opening should be made
large enough to insert the cushion and it is made in
the same way as a dress placket. (See Openings.) The
inside seams should be oversewn.

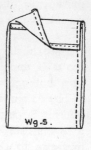

To make envelope type pillowcases fold the material
up wrong side out as in the diagram, with the flap
coming right over the top. Stitch the side seams.
When turned right side out the seams come inside the
top flap making it tidy.

Wg.s.

Curtains are most easily made with special
tape with cords threaded through it to pull
them up to the required degree of fullness.
Turn the top hem down to make a frill not
more than 2″ deep, otherwise it will flop over
in use. Place the tape to cover the raw edge

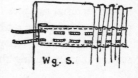

Wg. S.

and tack it. Machine each edge in place. Pull the cords up to the
required size and tie off securely.

Index